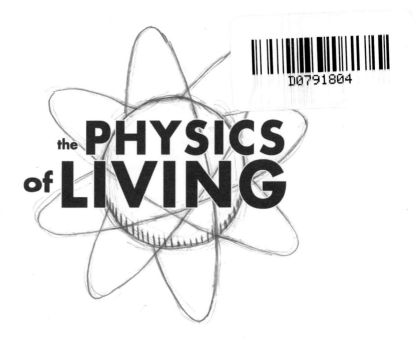

the **PHYSICS**
of **LIVING**

Also by Norman E. Amundson:

Amundson, N.E. *Active Engagement*

Amundson, N.E. *The Individual Style Survey*

Amundson, N.E. & Borgen, W.A. *At the controls: Charting a course through unemployment*

Amundson, N.E. & Poehnell, G. *Career Pathways*

Amundson, N.E. & Poehnell, G. *Career Pathways: Quick Trip*

Amundson, N.E., Poehnell, G. & Smithson, S. *Employment counselling theory and strategies: A book of readings*

Borgen, W.A. & Amundson, N.E. *The experience of unemployment*

Borgen, W.A., Pollard, D., Amundson, N.E. & Westwood, M. *Employment groups: The counselling connection*

McCormick, R., Amundson, A., & Poehnell, G. *Guiding Circles: An Aboriginal guide to finding career paths, Booklet 1: understanding yourself.*

Poehnell, G. & Amundson, N.E. *Career Crossroads: A personal career positioning system*

The Physics of Living

Norman E. Amundson, Ph.D.

University of British Columbia

THE PHYSICS OF LIVING

National Library of Canada Cataloguing in Publication

Amundson, Norman E. (Norman Edmund), 1948-
    The physics of living / Norman E. Amundson, Nick Frühling, Spence Frühling.

        Includes bibliographical references.
        ISBN 0-9684345-3-3

        1. Life. 2. Physics—Miscellanea. I. Frühling, Nick.
II. Frühling, Spence. III. Title.
BD431.A48 2003   128   C2002-911385-7

Published by Ergon Communications
To order this book or other Ergon Communication publications, contact:
        Ergon Communications
        3260 Springford Ave.
        Richmond, B.C. V7E 1T9 Canada
        Fax. (604) 448-9025
        Website: www.ergon-communications.com

Cover design and illustrations by Nick and Spence Frühling
Layout design by Gray Poehnell

Dedicated to my wife and best friend, Jeanette.

Together we seek to create a meaning-full life!

Acknowledgements

A book, like a performance, has a cast and credits that go beyond the work of the author. My wife, Jeanette, has been a constant source of support and inspiration during the writing of this book. She read numerous drafts of the manuscript and always provided constructive and encouraging feedback. Her work on the Balance Wheel was particularly helpful. She also made significant contributions to the ideas contained in the last chapter.

My friend and colleague, Gray Poehnell, also made a significant contribution to the manuscript. Over the years Gray and I have had many opportunities to discuss ideas during our bike rides along the Richmond dike. I am also very appreciative of Gray's technical and layout design efforts in the final preparation of the book.

Other reviewers of the book included Lynne Bezanson, Carl Leggo, Marla Arvay, Dan Stone, Andrew Thrift, and Søren Sørensen. I very much appreciate their suggestions and the encouragement I have received.

TABLE OF CONTENTS

x

1

LAYING THE TRACK

*... a desire to think about how one can live in the world
with wisdom, truth, and beauty ...*

*... addressing the broader issue of living a life,
a life filled to the brim with meaning and purpose,
a meaning-full life ...*

*... physical principles explored as metaphors
for the psychological world ...*

I have been involved in adult education and counsellor training for more than 25 years and in that time have published many academic and practical articles and books. As a professor, I enjoy writing; as a teacher, I also enjoy the next step of making complex topics understandable. As I think about the present project, however, I am aware that I am moving into a somewhat new domain. Physics had been one of my best subjects as a student; counselling psychology has been my profession. Bringing these two subject areas together brings the past into the present with the possibility of creating a new future. It comes from the desire to think about how one can live in the world with wisdom, truth, and beauty. It is a body, spirit, and mind issue.

The focus of my exploration has taken some new turns, pushing me beyond my usual comfort zone. Thankfully, I recently have had the opportunity for a sabbatical leave where there was time for reflective analysis and behavioral change. I have had to look inward as well as outward. I have taken time for reflection and have begun to pay particular attention to the voice of the spirit that exists at the centre of my being. I have included in my reading,

4

thinking, and doing both the spirit and the body. I have addressed topics that I usually gloss over.

I am painfully aware of my many shortcomings. Nevertheless, I would like to share some aspects of my journey with you. As with most writing projects, there is value for the writer as well as the reader. As I put some of these ideas on the printed page, there is a certain call to personal accountability; and, therefore, it is important for me not only to share ideas but also to try to live consistently with the ideas I express. Hopefully, some of these ideas will spur you on in your own journey.

5

This book is not written for any particular person or group. The ideas I am addressing here have relevance for people from many different walks of life. If you are aware of some of my earlier work, you will know that I have spent many years giving a voice to the experiences of unemployed people. More recently I have been examining the increasing challenges of working life. My purpose here is to move beyond the employment dimension to address the broader issue of living a life, a life filled to the brim with meaning and purpose, a meaning-full life. Hopefully the points that I make here will be relevant to you whatever your employment status.

As you read through the various sections of the book, you will note that different physical principles are covered

in each section. These considerations carried from the
traditional scientific world are laid down alongside the
psychological world. Physics also touches on matters of
spirituality, the great questions, and the search for God, as
understood and wrestled with by the great physicists. This
is a subject often neglected in the psychological field. I will
try to do some catching up in this particular work.

6

I have tried to write so that each chapter can be read
separately as well as within a more general context. The
second chapter focuses on the basic spatial coordinates of
matter, namely length, width, and depth. From this basic
structure comes a focus on these dimensions and how they
define the essence of our lives. In this chapter, I consider
how the three dimensions shed light on quality of life issues
and the search for balanced living. The third chapter
addresses the way in which matter moves through space,
sometimes as a ball (individual cause-and-effect properties)
and other times as a wave (the collective). In particular, I
examine the notion of life patterns, their uniqueness and
their collective identity. Various ways of assessing life
patterns are highlighted. In the fourth chapter, there is a
discussion of motion and how theory related to what
physics calls vectors and scalars helps to define the
magnitude, shape, and direction of one's life journey. Of
special interest here are the goals we set for ourselves, the

barriers that stand in the way, and the coping mechanisms we employ to overcome the challenges. The fifth chapter moves into the domain of quantum physics and provides a forum for issues related to complexity, paradox, uncertainty, flexibility, and action. In the sixth and seventh chapters, I shift the focus to energy as the source for heat transfer and electricity. Within this context, there are issues related to generating empathy, as well as burnout and energy flow. In the concluding chapter, water, simple H_2O, becomes a metaphor for three key concepts—hope, heroes, and opportunity—and how these ideas are closely connected to the process of making life changes.

Each chapter begins with a basic physical principle. Each principle is described and some general observations are made. These observations are then engaged as metaphors in the psychological world. Finally, a number of different exercises focus specifically on personal applications. In this way, the book can be used as a form of self-exploration, as well as a journey into the possibility of physics for living. You are welcome to walk alongside.

2

SPACE-TIME

DIMENSIONS

... focusing on the length of life (a time dimension),
the busyness of living that helps to define width,
and the purpose, meaning, and depth
that helps to define the spiritual part of our being ...

... our values and the meanings we make
impact all of the dimensions of our lives ...

...one of the goals of pursuing three-dimensional living
is to configure boundaries in such a way
as to find balance ...

In the physical world, events occur at a particular time and at a particular point in space (Hawking, 1988). These events can be specified using four numbers or coordinates for the dimensions of length, width, depth (or height), and time. Albert Einstein's theory of relativity does not distinguish between these dimensions, and such renowned physicists as Stephen Hawking acknowledge that it is hard to visualize space using these coordinates. However, to the untrained mind, the physical world as four-dimensional is simply the image of cubes and clocks that we encounter on a day-to-day basis. I am going to simplify the structure even further by including time under the designation of "length." Thus, I will simply be referring to the dimensions of length, width, and depth.

It would seem to me that some psychological parallels can be drawn between these measurement dimensions and the way in which we live our lives. Specifically I am referring to the ways in which we focus on the **length** of life (a time dimension), the busyness of living that helps to define **width**, and the purpose, meaning, and **depth** that help to address the spiritual part of our being. I will start by describing each of the dimensions.

The dimensions of our lives do not function independently but rather work together to create wholeness in our being. The values we hold and the meanings we make impact all of the dimensions of our lives. It is important to keep this perspective in mind when looking at each of these dimensions.

The Dimension of Length

11

Length, our first dimension, appears at a first glance to be the most concrete measurement; it is something we measure with a degree of certainty or objectivity. We count hours, days, months, years, and so on to define just about everything we do, from the length of a conversation—"I just have to make a five minute call"—to the length of time we walk on this earth. But is time really the uniform measurement of sunrise and sunset that a clock denotes or that seasons and calendars depict as our journey around the sun? We experience time "speeding up" and "slowing down"; it is a commodity that some "spend," others "waste," and still others "save" (Wujec, 1995). When I was younger, I couldn't imagine "running out of time." Some people always seem to run out of time, while others always seem to be creating new ways of finding time. At 2 years of age, one year represented one half of my life; at 10, one year had become a measure of only 10% of my life; at 50, a year has been further reduced to 2% of my experience. Now that I have passed the half-century mark, the years feel shorter and shorter as time relentlessly moves on. I have no doubt that our perception of time is as subjective as it is objective, and it is in the interplay between these two realities that we are called to create meaning-full lives.

An important aspect of physically defining length of life is the extent to which we make the most of the time that we are given. An interesting question to ponder is the anticipated length of our life. Some will want to stretch this further and ask that if life on earth is the embodiment of a soul, does life even end with the physical shutting down of our bodies? Our answers to these questions help to define our experience of living and what we are willing to put into our life to give it meaning. As human beings, how far do we stretch our life and to what end?

In many respects our expectations about time help to define where we put our energy. Time itself has three components, past, present, and future. Some people focus primarily towards the future; others become fixated on the past, losing sight of both present and future possibilities. With three choices for each moment of time we are given, we need here to learn to live with balance even within the dimensions. We are given the present; and joy is found as

12

we live in the fullness of the moment, as we experience the wisdom, the truth, and the beauty of what is. For some, the greatest search of a lifetime is to know how to create or discover and hold onto the joy-filled moments in the midst of a very broken world. And all the while not losing sight of the past or the future. Our great common gift is choice about the meaning that we assign to our life experiences.

There are so many different ways of enhancing or diminishing our lives. When one thinks about length of life, the most obvious sources are the choices we make about how we treat our bodies, what we eat and drink, the air we breathe, and the exercise we participate in or avoid. Psychological stresses also have the power to impact the dimensions of length (taking into consideration subjectivity and objectivity, past, present, and future) in our life. Making healthy choices helps to lengthen our physical lives and also to enhance the quality of living. These words are easy to write, and yet for most of us are the hardest to put into action. I used to think it was lack of discipline but now recognize that it is more about what I consider to be important. I often find myself looking right past the basic needs of my body as I hurry on to the next task; I fail to pay attention to what my body is telling me. Our body certainly tries to speak into our lives; we need to take the time to make room for this conversation. Sometimes we need the help of doctors, health professionals, or just other caring individuals to get us to the point of hearing and responding appropriately to the messages that our body is trying to give us. As we learn to live well with the dimensions of length, we find that not only is the length of our lives affected but also the quality of that length.

The Dimension of Width

As soon as the discussion shifts to the quality of living, we start to move into the second dimension, the breadth or width of our life as defined by involvement in a wide range of activities. We are involved in activity through the range of roles that we assume in work, in leisure, and in family or community life. Our various forms of involvement broaden our lives by providing stimulation (mental, physical, and spiritual), supportive relationships, meaning, and structure to every dimension. As we fully engage in life, we are called upon to participate in various arenas and these activities can be personally rewarding and meaningful.

This expanded involvement enables us to reach beyond our personal needs and to begin to address the needs of others. By extending ourselves in this way, we multiply goodness and also enrich our personal lives. One of the mysteries of life is how we most often gain more by helping others than through our own efforts to help ourselves. We all have a basic need to feel that we "matter," that our lives are important, not only to ourselves but also to others (Schlossberg, Lynch, & Chickering, 1989). The power of mattering can be felt whenever we find ourselves in a situation where we don't matter, where we are made to feel invisible, undervalued, or marginalized. Our sense of self-worth depends as much on how we are treated by others as on our own personal attitudes. By reaching out to others, we have the possibility of building mattering in the lives of others as well as in our own lives. It is this sense of mattering that gives meaning to the activities we enter into.

15

These activities provide width, put us into community, and, in that context, have the potential to be immensely satisfying. At the same time, as with any communal structure, there are people and situations that pose problems. These problems can take many shapes; there can be situations where there is too much activity and other times when there is not enough. I want to look in both of these directions, beginning first with over-involvement.

Our involvement in the activities around us has the potential to become a kind of status symbol that defines our importance in the community. Moses (1999) talks about the "cult of busyness" and suggests that we use busyness like a badge of honour to reflect our status in the modern workplace. In response to the question "How are things going?" we moan and groan about our busyness, while at the same time feeling self-assured about our identity and importance. The underlying message is that surely someone that busy must be important, must have value. Even when we know that we are hurting ourselves through excessive busyness, we continue because there are both external and internal rewards. From that inner voice of wisdom, we recognize that an excess of quantity reduces the quality we all desire not only in this dimension but also in the dimensions of length and depth.

There are many ways of metaphorically expressing this excess of activity in our lives. Saltzman (1991) uses the image of the automobile and talks about the shifting of gears and the need to learn to gear our lives to our own natural rhythms, rhythms that are of course different for each individual. As I have considered this situation, a number of other images have come to mind. I have thought about a simple elastic band and what happens when it is stretched too far. Even if it doesn't break, the elasticity is lost over a period of time. Another image came to me on a recent visit to my chiropractor. My attention was drawn to the model of a skeleton that hung by her door. As I contemplated this intricate arrangement of bones, I could see a small sponge carefully placed between each set of bones. The intervertebral discs in the spine, with the help of ligaments, act as a cushion between the bones, thus enabling movement in the body. I was well aware of the effects of the breakdown of these cushions in my own body. As a metaphor for living well in the dimension of width, we can think of "down time" as the lubricant that facilitates movement. Without this lubricant there is going to be friction and, therefore, pain. One final way of looking at this down time is from the context of the Jewish tradition. Here we see the concept of a Sabbath, one day in seven that is set aside to honour the Creator and to follow in the path of the Creator as we rest from our work. This focus on rest becomes the truth, the lubricant that enables us to live well in all the dimensions. My own experience of the need for rest came as a gift, a dream, or perhaps a vision of sorts. I found myself lifted up to a higher place of being, a quiet place in the forest, with a blanket of snow and a fire burning brightly. In this place of seeing, I experienced the wisdom, the beauty, and the truth of a light that was beyond my ability to grasp, and yet compelled me to look on it. In the flames I saw and heard voices of praise and I felt the presence of an overwhelming power. As I walked back to the city, I asked myself why more people couldn't see what I had just seen. The answer came back: "They do not seek out the quiet places."

Stacking activities together without sufficient breaks is not the only way to create excess. In addition to general busyness, we have to be aware of the types of activities in which we are engaged. Doing too much of any one thing can create its own problems. I always remember the last part of my doctoral program when I was waiting to collect my research data. This waiting meant that I basically had a summer free of obligations. I decided to devote my time to tennis. While this lofty goal sounded great at the beginning of the summer, by the end it was not really that much fun; and surprisingly, my game didn't improve that much. I became bored, tired of the same activity day in and day out. I longed for a meaning for what I did and some variety in the activity. Living well isn't just about filling our life with activity; there is also a need for variety and meaning.

At its best, a life rich in activity signals a life rich in meaning. Our lives are meant to be "meaning-full." The problems come when we either have too much activity with too little "meaning-fullness" or a meaning that exists in other people's minds more than in our own. There are also the problems associated with simply too little activity. The absence of activity does not necessarily translate into leisure. Lack of activity can slow the passing of time and create its own form of pain and stress. Many wish with all their heart that the phone would ring, that there would be an offer of activity or work to be done of any kind. Most seek ultimately for meaningful work, activities that begin to stretch the width of their lives into the dimension of depth.

The Dimension of Depth

The third and perhaps most significant dimension is that of depth, finding purpose and meaning in life. Most significant because it is here that we begin to know ourselves, to know who we are, what we believe and believe in. It is also a most significant dimension because it is from this place that we can also truly begin to know that which is not ourselves but that which is the other, whether that other be other persons or things, or ideas, or the possibility of God. The process of finding our spiritual selves can come in many ways. As a young teen I was involved in a serious electrical accident; one of my friends died in my arms but somehow I survived. I suffered burns but I was alive. Not only was I alive, I also was able later to have children despite the possibility of sterility in these types of accidents. This experience of surviving a serious electrical accident spoke to me of a purpose for living. That event turned my focus to the spiritual and to a relationship with God that could be personal. I determined to make my life count. Awakened to the spiritual dimension of my life's journey, I began looking for the joy-full moments of each new day that were one signal to me of the spiritual relationship that was a part of this dimension.

The conclusions we come to may differ; the common point from a psychological perspective is the need to make sense of our lives. The call to meaning and purpose is strong; and in our own unique ways, we seek to find the answers to the deeper questions: What is life? Who am I? How did I come to be here? Where am I going? Where, if anywhere, are we as a civilization going—particularly in the face of ongoing global conflict? How should we live with one another? How can we best respond to the world around us?

It has already been noted that the meaning we ascribe to our lives has a significant impact on the dimensions of width and length. At the most basic level, our life purpose (why am I here?) strengthens us and gives us an added perspective on the challenges we face. It affects the choices we make and the resolve that we have in carrying out our plans. One of the best-known studies of this resolve can be found in the life and work of Victor Frankl (1963). His struggle and courage in a World War II concentration camp reflected his search for meaning and purpose, even under the most appalling conditions. In the psychological world, his work on meaning is best understood as Logotherapy, the will to meaning. Other disciplines and individuals approach the question of meaning of life and purpose from their own contexts.

Dimensional Configurations

Contained within these three dimensions are opportunities for wholeness. Yet even in living three-dimensionally, it is possible to experience a variety of configurations or patterns. The best of these configurations provides for well-balanced living. Others create distortions and warp our lives in ways that are less healthy.

In this segment I will be describing some of the more problematic configurations that might emerge. There are undoubtedly many different configurations that could be described; I will simply illustrate some of the more common characteristics associated with a loss of balance. Each of these problematic configurations and whatever others you may discover in your own search for balance tend to have both an active and a passive nature. Some people make choices and through their actions end up in a problematic configuration. Others find themselves within a similar problematic configuration because of their inability to respond appropriately.

Problems with Length

1. Skinny Living

People who find themselves in this configuration are strongly over-emphasizing the length dimension. They are very concerned about living a long life, and most of their activities seem to follow this singular focus. A diminishing involvement in other outside activities can lay a foundation for a rather narrow (skinny) view of living. Preserving the "self" becomes the main event. Some utilize an active response and try to hold on to their youth through diet, fitness, and any number of medical procedures and "medicines." For others, there is a more passive response. In this frame of mind, people constantly find themselves worrying about every ache and change in bodily function. Falling into this lifestyle preoccupation is particularly easy in later life. This passive focus usually begins with the onset of a particular health problem and then becomes generalized through worry to life itself.

2. Extreme Living

In recent years there has been a rapid increase in interest in what has been called "extreme sports." The thrill for many young people and some older people as well is the testing of physical limits in high-risk situations. It may be something like skiing out of bounds, kayaking down waterfalls, or biking down the sides of mountains. Whatever the activity, the emphasis is on experiencing life at its outer limits, on the edge. The greater the adrenaline rush, the higher the risk; the more extreme the experience, the better. While there is at one level a caution that involves a myriad of safety equipment and procedures, it is followed at another level by a reckless abandon about preservation that seems to question even the value of life itself. From this perspective the focus is on living in the present moment; the dimension that would speak of length of life seems to go unheard. Passively, extreme living would apply to many persons eking out an existence at the edge of society and its social structures. The drug culture, street people, and the homeless are living with self-neglect and extremes that are physically costly. Whether by choice or circumstance, they are living at a level that places them in continual risk.

Problems with Width

3. Stubby Living

With this configuration there is an overabundance of activity with little regard to the quality and length of life. Long hours, lack of sleep, constant stress, fast food, and a reliance on alcohol and/or drugs to keep going helps to set the stage for future problems. In this state of affairs, there is little time to "stop and smell the roses." Constant motion, and for some workaholism, creates its own set of problems for both social relationships and physical and mental health. Some actively seek out a constant "buzz"; others search for activity to avoid what is too difficult to face; while still others prefer a scale of activity that provides an abundance of superficial recognition without ever having to consider depth dimension questions. Passively, stubby living is more a matter of circumstance. Many find themselves caught in work situations with limited resources and a never-ending stream of work. (Working single parents with young families are perhaps the greatest single group in this category in developed countries.) The overall effect is a growing sense of despair and hopelessness.

4. Sideline Living

This configuration contrasts sharply with stubby living. In this configuration, there is a definite lack of activity. Life events, such as unemployment, retirement, health or a disability, sideline many at various times. Others just can't seem to make a move, perhaps afraid of making a mistake or of being rejected by others. Some live forever waiting for someone else to initiate their involvement in life's possibilities. And then there are those few who actively withdraw from the life we have tended to call "normal," as they choose solitude, silence, and space as their most constant companions. However, for most people who could be described as living on the sidelines, this is not a chosen place and they would love to be more involved. For them, a lack of involvement over time has a negative impact on feelings of self-worth and can also serve to diminish degrees of motion and flexibility. The danger in staying too long in this category is the development of a too strong "victim" mentality.

Problems with Depth

5. False-Front Living

In many of the smaller towns that were well characterized in the early Western movies, buildings took on a grand appearance by the use of false fronts and grand entrances. More recently a Southern Hemisphere city attempted to preserve its heritage sights by keeping only the front exterior walls and entrances, with nothing behind or perhaps a new structure taking the place of the old. It was not well received and soon was abandoned as an architectural option. In both of these stories, the buildings looked large and luxurious from the street level. Once past these walls and doors, however, there was emptiness or some other incongruent reality. The same applies to many people's lives. From the outside they may look terrific; there appears to be plenty of activity and things seem to move smoothly. Scratching the surface, however, of those who have actively pursued a false-front lifestyle reveals a superficiality that expresses very little depth and often a hidden lack of self-care. More passively, false-front living

26 simply reveals an emptiness that often longs to be filled. This more passive false-front living is most often the domain of those who have not had the opportunities that would allow them to consider how to add depth to their lives or who have let those opportunities slip by. For both, the end result is a tragic superficiality that nonetheless can be used rather effectively to hide from other people and even from oneself.

6. Single-Issue Living

The adage about "one-trick ponies" comes to mind when describing this particular configuration. While having strength in the depth dimension is certainly a major asset, it also can be overdone if people become fixated on one issue or in one direction and spend all their time and energy focused on what becomes their cause. Meaning and purpose are meant to nurture and enrich our lives (both

width and length) and should be incorporated into living
in a holistic sense. This does not mean that having
particular causes or a specific mission is not a legitimate life
choice. The focus rather is on those who either become
actively involved and gradually obsessive and compulsive
about a particular cause or those who more passively have
developed such a narrow range or focus that they have lost
their peripheral vision. In both cases, the cause or mission
serves as an escape or as an excuse for not facing life's other
responsibilities. Again, it is the matter of balance that must
be taken into account.

27

Problems with Overall Configuration

7. Bandwagon Living

As with false-front living, there is a real superficiality
here. The difference is that the configuration keeps
changing. Persons with this configuration keep shifting
their boundaries to accommodate current fashions in any
dimension, wanting to catch and ride each new
bandwagon. A definite shape and a modicum of stability to
that shape is lacking. Here we meet people who are very
sincere in what they are doing but can't be counted upon
for any sustained action. Their passion is short lived; they
can adopt seemingly inconsistent positions on any number

of life issues. From a passive stance, bandwagon living is simply lacking a will or a clear path to follow. Those who haven't developed the ability to think for themselves or who have found no satisfactory rock on which to plant their feet and future are swept along by the tides of change.

8. Stuck-in-a-Rut Living

This configuration is the complete opposite of Bandwagon Living. From this perspective, people just can't seem to make any life changes. In contrast to those who live with a single issue or cause, this group is often dissatisfied with the way things are going but seem to lack the fortitude to change their circumstances. This inertia is passive by nature and seems connected to a lack of initiative, fear, being overly cautious, or perhaps life events such as poor health. Others appear to be more active, speaking of change, even making resolutions for change but very rarely actually creating any movement. Those who fit this description are most often repeating messages that they have received from others about the need to change. They have heard "you should" for most of their life, so that they are the best "should-ers" you will find; but very rarely are they "doers." Finally, there are those who have grown so accustomed to their particular "rut" that it begins to seem normal; it becomes a place they choose; and so they no longer make any effort to change; nor have they any desire to change. The ruts have become comfortable.

Life Balance

One of the goals of pursuing three-dimensional living is to configure boundaries in such a way as to find balance. In a fast-moving world there are many forces pulling and pushing in different ways. Having the attitude and the skills to manoeuver through turbulent waters requires a form of ongoing watchfulness. Balance must be actively pursued.

The component parts for balanced living include self-knowledge, empathy for others, self-confidence, information, problem solving, communication skills, creativity, courage, and action planning. These factors combined with individual identity, personality, and unique life experiences leave little room for formulas. We all have different balance points and, therefore, need to determine the configuration that works best for us.

Life balance within the dimensions of length, width, and depth touches every aspect of our life. There are many indicators when life is out of balance. One obvious example is the work situation. Many people find themselves trapped in work situations where they are experiencing a form of career malaise. Some are on the road to career burnout; while others have profound doubts about the meaning of the work they are doing. Moses (1997, p. 105) describes career distress and those who experience it as follows:

- Feeling out of control, unable to make predictions about the future: they see little relationship between what they do and what happens to them.

30

- No sense of personal satisfaction: they are not finishing work at the level they would like. They feel they are not making a meaningful contribution.

- Self-confidence has been eroded: they are beginning to question their competence and feel they are losing their "edge." They worry about the future.

- They are cynical about their employers, and pessimistic about their futures.

This state of career malaise characterizes only too well a lack of meaning and balance in life. Lest we think that despair is our only companion, let me say this state of affairs is not the end of the road. As we take time to examine the various dimensions of living, and our place within those dimensions, there are endless possibilities for a more positive future than the one just described. It is our choice whether or not to engage those possibilities.

Assessing Life Balance

This section is designed as a self-assessment guide to help with the identification of life balance or imbalance, as the case may be. If one part of life is out of balance, it will interfere with functioning in other areas. Take the time for reflection as you complete the life balance assessment exercises.

At a general level, you may want to try making a three-dimensional drawing (length, width, depth) that captures your feeling of proportion in each of these domains. Sometimes it is helpful to just put it down on paper. What would be the relative size and shape of each dimension for you. When I tried this exercise, I found it helpful to use a ten-point scale to represent each dimension; you may have other ideas. Try sketching your picture in the space below.

My 3D Living Drawing

Life Balance Wheel

A second exercise, which is more specific, is based on a Life Balance Wheel (in Poehnell & Amundson, 2001) developed by my wife, Jeanette. This wheel, pictured below, has four sets of contrasting factors: work and play, physical and spiritual, social and personal, and emotional and intellectual. For illustration purposes, the wheel has been completed. The shaded areas reflect the extent (too much, just right, too little) to which the various dimensions are experienced.

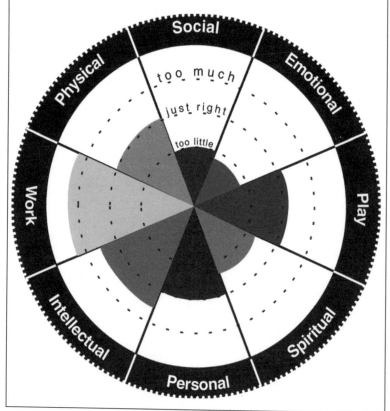

These factors are defined as follows:

1. **Work** – what I do as vocation, or occupation (paid or unpaid); how I earn a living or prepare to earn a living at some future date.
2. **Play** – recreation including hobbies, music and the arts, and friendship; activities that I do on my own or with friends that bring me pleasure and rest.
3. **Personal** – time spent on my own; time given to reflection, knowing myself, and following my own paths.
4. **Social** – time spent in the company of others, in work or play; contributing to and taking into consideration the welfare / well-being of other persons or of a group.
5. **Intellectual** – activities that challenge my mind; thinking activities such as time spent reading about ideas and practices, gathering and remembering information, solving problems, and trying out new ideas.
6. **Emotional** – engaging in relationships and other activities that encourage me to experience and express feelings and to develop my ability to have appropriate feelings and not just ideas about the world; sympathy and empathy.
7. **Physical** – taking care of my body; using my body to experience the world around me; thinking and acting in ways that promote health.
8. **Spiritual** – perspective taking; knowing my place in the world, with other people, and in relation to truth, beauty, and wisdom; developing a sense of the meaning of my life, taking time to know and experience what I believe is true.

How does your life balance wheel look? When you assess each dimension in the light of your own life (too much, too little, just right), what kind of a wheel have you created? Is it balanced enough to give you a fairly smooth ride, or is it full of bumps? If it is full of bumps and if you know the ride that you experience as your life is quite rough at the moment, continue on with the following exercises; they may assist in helping you find more balance. Even if your wheel is relatively smooth, the exercises that follow provide a good tune up.

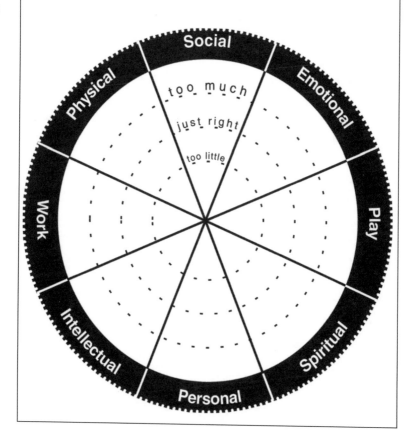

Things I Like to Do

As a starting point to assess life balance, you might want to think about what you really like to do (at home, in your leisure time, and/or at work), whether or not you are doing them at this time in you life. If you were to make a list, what would be on that list? Fill out the form below. Begin by simply trying to list at least 20 activities. The things you list do not have to be profound—this is for your own self-reflection. Perhaps you enjoy taking a bath, reading, playing tennis, studying rocks, etc. Let your mind wander and try to write down items as they come to mind.

35

Things I Like to Do	A	B	C	D
1.				
2.				
3.				
4.				
5.				
6.				
7.				

Things I Like to Do	A	B	C	D
8.				
9.				
10.				
11.				
12.				
13.				
14.				
15.				
16.				
17.				
18.				
19.				
20.				

Look over the items that you have listed. Think about each of the items according to the following questions. The answers to these questions can be recorded in the columns to the right of the list you have made.

A. How long has it been since you have done the activity?
B. What are the costs associated with doing the activity?
C. What is the involvement of other people in the activity?
D. What does each activity tap into on the Life Balance Wheel?

What insights come to you when you look at these activities in some depth? Is there anything on your list that you love to do but haven't done for a long time? What is keeping you from doing the activity? Many people find that most of the items on their list cost little or no money; is that the case for you? How much involvement do you have with other people, and who are the other people? How balanced are the activities that you enjoy doing? Do you find yourself with too many activities focused in a particular domain, and what might that tell you about yourself? The space below is for you to write your personal reflections.

Personal Reflections

Now that you have read this chapter and these activities, is there anything that you would like to change in your life? Take a moment to think about where you are now and then shift to what your life would look like if you made the necessary changes. Usually we sit with our problems and look at all the barriers. Try something different! Suppose that instead of starting with the problem, you started with the solution (with a wheel that is balanced rather than bent—metaphorically speaking). Don't worry about how you are going to get there; just feel the smoothness of the ride. Once you can feel this solution, look again at the problem. Does the problem look any different from a solution perspective? What steps would you have taken to give yourself a smoother ride? If you now want to make some changes in your life, take the time to write down what you want to change. Think carefully about what specifically you are going to do and whether this is in fact a realistic plan. Remember that all good plans start with a first step. Also, share what you are planning with at least one other person, an encourager. Changes are usually best made with support from others.

Action Plan

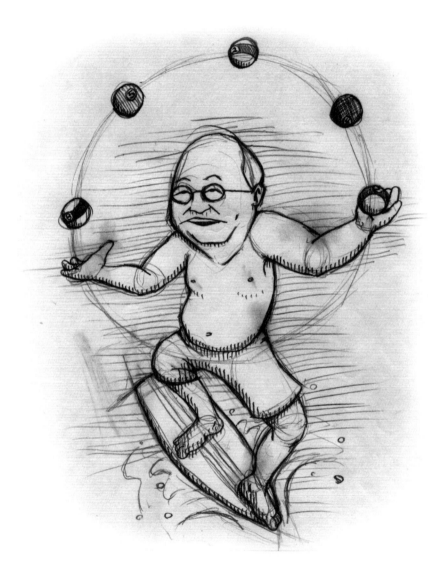

3

BILLIARD BALLS
AND WAVES

... we each have a separate, unique, and individual identity
but at the same time, are members of a community ...

... the constellation of patterns that exist
in the psyche of a person, our individual identity,
is a form of 'psychological DNA' ...

... immersion within groups helps
to provide shape and direction to our lives;
the groups that surround us impact
our sense of identity ...

Within the metaphor of matter, it is interesting to take from physics the notion that when we think about movement, there are two very different models that emerge. In one instance, it seems that matter operates like billiard balls. Separate boundaries are evident and the connections reflect a straightforward cause and effect relationship. One ball is struck and moves in a certain direction at a specific speed, strikes other balls or hard surfaces; this interaction of the ball changes its direction and speed, and in turn sets other balls in motion. That is one kind of movement; one we are all familiar with whether it be billiard balls or any one of a myriad of cause-and-effect relationships in the natural world.

At other times, however, a very different model of movement emerges. Rather than a billiard ball action, it seems that matter fuses together and operates more like a wave. There is a shift from the physics of particles to a physics modeled according to the collectivity of particles. This grouping phenomenon leads to wave theories and gives us different models to reflect particular aspects of physical reality. And to further complicate matters, quantum physics can also point to times when waves will act as particles and particles will respond as waves. The same can be said of the psychological realm. At times we seem to reflect a more individual orientation and at other times adopt a more collective approach. It is not that one view is more correct than the other is. We hold within ourselves the capacity for both individual action and collective identity.

To understand more fully the motion of living and being, we need to be aware of the interplay between the individual and the collective. We each have a separate, unique, and individual identity but at the same time are members of a community. To fully understand ourselves, we need to have a perspective that looks at the individual but also recognizes the importance of factors such as culture, gender, social class, family dynamics, and so on. To hold both of these realities involves thinking and living not in terms of an "either-or" but rather with a "both-and" construction (Gelatt, 1989).

Since we seem to have these two identities, how do they develop and change with the passage of time, and perhaps more importantly, how can we come to know the nature of both our individual and collective identity? These are topics that have generated a lot of speculation and research. The various social sciences, theology, and the natural sciences connect here; like particles of light, these form a wave, which hopefully will lead us towards a better understanding of human nature and how to best live in the world. And somehow, in the mist of all that is, each person also has a unique identity to discover and nurture.

Development of the Individual and the Collective Identity

44

There are, of course, many perspectives on the development of identity. I have been impressed by the work of the attachment theorists (Bowlby, 1969/1982; 1973; 1980; Ainsworth, 1989) who address the importance of positive early relationships in healthy identity development. A secure early relationship helps to set a tone and a pattern for future relationships and contributes to both individual and collective identity. The secure relationship helps to reduce anxiety, establish trust, build self-confidence, and provide a base for exploratory behaviors. Without this security there is vulnerability, dependence, and emotional instability. There is good research support for attachment theory. Lopez (1995, p. 401) reports that "early attachment classification does appear to be at least moderately predictive of the child's later emotional and social adjustment, with *secure* children demonstrating greater emotional self-regulation during difficult problem-solving tasks, more appropriate use of adult support, and greater empathic and cooperative orientations than their insecurely attached peers."

When one considers the importance of the attachment bond, it is important to avoid an overly narrow definition of attachment relationships (Bartholomew & Thompson, 1995). While early parenting seems to play the most significant role, there are also other attachment relationships that can be considered. There are situations in which other family members or even peers provide significant attachment experiences. It is also noteworthy that persons who are spiritually well connected describe a relationship that meets basic attachment needs. We begin with the initial parental bond and let other attachment relationships emerge on our journey.

Both our individual and collective identities come from a common source— significant attachment relationships. In many ways they are simply flip sides of the same coin. Nevertheless they do have very different shapes and need to be considered separately.

Individual Identity

The establishment of an individual identity depends on a process called individuation or differentiation. It is important not to confuse individuation with individualism. Individuation is a developmental process that helps to shape and mold personal identity, always with the knowledge that although we are individuals, we live connected to others. Individuation allows persons to see themselves, to see others, and, then, to take into account that others also can see them. The key here is interdependence. Individualism, on the other hand, is a description of the way in which some people focus on the individual self to the exclusion of the group. I see and know myself as the centre point; how others see me is of little concern. Recognition of others and their value has only secondary significance. Independence is primary.

46

Individuation / differentiation in relationships is clearly the more desirable ongoing life process. It has as its focus the development of a functionally unique personal identity. Achieving this end often involves some struggle. From a developmental perspective, one can think of the young children whose assertions of "no" are the beginning of a discovery about their own person and limits. In teenage years, this struggle seems to come to the forefront again with renewed energy and power. I can remember looking at our own children during this teenage phase. After a number of very peaceful and collaborative years, life was changing for them again and, therefore, also for us. Out of this more turbulent time, we witnessed and continue to witness the emergence of three vibrant young adults with their own identity not only in relation to parents and family but also in relation to peers and culture. And so it goes! The struggle for individuation / differentiation is an ongoing life process, and it can be observed at every step of the life journey.

Problems in living occur when the efforts being made toward individuation / differentiation are blocked. In this scenario we have the emergence of fused relationships. A fused relationship is characterized by lack of flexibility and excessive dependence. It may be useful here to develop another metaphor from our earlier metaphor concerning the arrangement of the bones in our back. The bones are organized so that there is some separation between them and in this gap are cartilage and ligaments (intervertebral discs). These "spaces" between the bones provide the ideal conditions for flexibility. In the same way, the individuation / differentiation process is similar to the development of the necessary spacing between the individual and other members of the group, usually family or friends but sometimes also workmates. Without this lubricant and space, there is not enough separation between people and this results in fused relationships. The defining characteristic of the fused relationship is the dependence on

47

THE PHYSICS OF LIVING

the other person to define identity. It is a situation where people seek out the collective identity (wave) prior to the healthy development of an individual identity or when the individual identity (billiard ball) is more appropriate.

Collective Identity

The second process in identity development focuses more on our connection within the group. This identity too is capable of growth and change and so needs to be considered developmentally. Carl Jung talks about the "collective unconscious" and suggests that there are bigger life forces that help to define our identity. One of the richest sources of imagery for an individual's collective identity comes out of images from Christian spirituality. Here one finds the collective identity imagined as the people of God, the city of God, the body of Christ, branches of one vine, sheep of one pasture or one shepherd, etc., alongside an individual personal relationship and responsibility. Our collective or wave identity exists at one level as a metaphysical force giving definition to our place in the group. At another level, collective identity is quite practical, calling for reflection, thoughtfulness, and action as we learn to live and work within social groups.

BILLIARD BALLS AND WAVES

The development of a practical, interpersonal awareness is something that occurs through social interaction. We learn from one another how to behave in the group, how to solve problems, and how to evaluate new situations. Some of the early psychological experiments come to mind in this regard. In one classic experiment, the judgment of the length of a line is affected by the feedback received from others. Group pressure is applied and many people alter their initial judgments. I have observed this group phenomenon many times through my work in career counselling. In one situation, a group member who was not a member of the dominant culture was trying to find her place in the group. She was free spirited and it was obvious at times that this style bothered some group members. After some time together, there was an equally obvious reduction in free-spirited behavior and in some instances the changes were quite dramatic. Nothing was said verbally, but certain looks would be manifest. An eyebrow was raised in disapproval and the effect was immediately noticeable.

The need for a collective identity is obvious; we live our lives in community and need to develop the skills and sensitivity to move successfully within this context. While we need to successfully separate ourselves from others, we also need to learn how to build and maintain meaningful relationships. Much of the traditional North American literature has focused on the individual without sufficient regard to the building and maintenance of the group; this focus results in what we described earlier as individualism rather than individuation. One of the reasons for this skewed perspective has been the over reliance on research that addresses the experiences of men rather than women (Goldberger, Tarule, Clinchy & Belenky, 1996). There are some strong gender differences in career development and one of the most obvious is the emphasis placed on relationships. For women, the development of relationships seems to be at least as important as the development of career independence.

Healthy career development is more than just "climbing a ladder." Certainly it is important to develop a positive momentum, but of equal importance are the meaningful relationships that are formed as part of the journey. Again, we are back to the issue of balance. The question is not whether to focus on career independence or relationships; both are integral parts of the career development process. For well-rounded healthy development, there is a need for both collective and individual development for both men and women.

This emphasis on relationships and the collective identity is also of prime importance in a cross-cultural context (Trompenaars, 1993). I have had the opportunity in recent years to work in many different cultural contexts and recently had the opportunity to help develop a career workbook for the aboriginal community (McCormick, Amundson, & Poehnell, 2002). The value of family and community is something that many different cultural groups share. The balance between individuation and the interpersonal is set at different levels depending on the various characteristics of different cultural groups. As people move across groups, these differences become apparent. Living in a large multicultural city, I have become aware of the adjustment difficulties associated with a shift in cultural context. For many new immigrants, there is nothing more disheartening than viewing the shift in young people away from the collective to a more individualistic perspective. On the other hand, there are also examples of oppressive control where people cry out for individual identity and freedom. I remember working in a college setting where some women were having serious difficulties in their families because of their desire to learn English and acquire skill training, appropriate behaviors within one culture but quite threatening and unacceptable to another. It is not an easy task, but essential, to remember in such situations the importance of balance and sensitivity to contextual factors. Cross-cultural interactions

51

and relationships remind us that even in the ordinary and the mundane we live a collective as well as individual identity. Socially, we become part of trends that are often set far from our borders. Something as simple and seemingly personal as the clothes we wear or the food we eat most likely began as an idea in someone else's mind or cultural style. As we become a part of that mindset, we, in turn, can set in motion a way of being that has the potential to create a whole range of economic and political waves.

52

Understanding Patterns of Individual and Collective Identity

As a starting point to examine individual identity, it is sometimes helpful to think about the many "selves" that make up the whole. While we tend to think of ourselves as single entities there is some evidence for the existence of multiple selves (Markus & Nurius, 1986; Martz, 2001). This has nothing to do with mental illness but rather the simple recognition that we can act in different ways at different times and in different places depending on circumstances. Each of us has our own unique constellation of selves. As I thought about my personal selves, I came up with the following list; yours may be different:

- Oliver Twist: "stocking up" when things are free
- Florence Nightingale: taking care of people who are hurting
- Jack Hammer: blasting others when frustrated
- Picasso: coming up with imaginative solutions
- Tiny Tim: fearing physical harm or the wrath of others
- Noble Warrior: taking a courageous stand on issues
- The Bumbler: lacking confidence when working with mechanics
- Pollyanna: endless energy and optimism

53

These selves cover a range of emotions and actions; some are positive while others are less desirable. There are some like "Tiny Tim" that are perhaps appropriate in some situations and not so helpful in others.

Possible Selves

What are some of the selves that you can see in yourself? List them in the space provided.

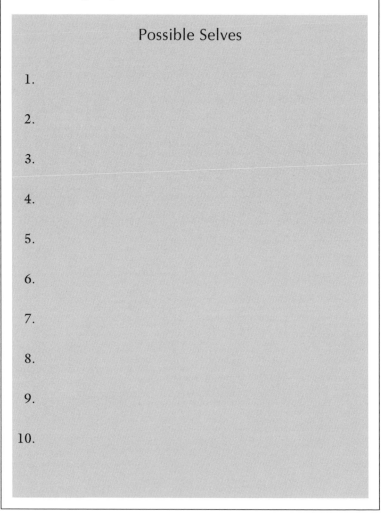

Possible Selves

1.

2.

3.

4.

5.

6.

7.

8.

9.

10.

Are there some selves that need to be held back while others need to be encouraged?

If you are facing a particular problem, what alternate perspectives can these different selves provide?

How do you decide which self is the most appropriate for a particular situation?

If you look at identity from a more holistic view, you can see many basic and individual life/career patterns embedded not only within the activities we enjoy but also in those that we may not enjoy (Amundson, 1998). Miller and Mattson (1989) make the point that each of us has a unique design that remains consistent throughout life. In the physical world, DNA is the name given to describe the unique pattern that is common to every tissue and cell in a body. I use the term "psychological DNA" to refer to the constellation of patterns that exist in the psyche of a person, our individual identity.

56

Psychological DNA

Our DNA patterns can be identified through in-depth analysis of life experiences. With this detailed analysis, I think it is particularly important to examine likes and dislikes. The likes provide insight into the positive nature of our psychological DNA; the dislikes demonstrate how we will respond when that potential is interrupted or when that positive nature is thwarted.

If you are interested in following through with this type of in-depth, Psychological DNA analysis take a moment to complete the following exercise. This is an activity that is good to do with a partner who can take notes for you as you tell your story and be reflective with you as you look for insights. It is also an activity where a counsellor can be of assistance. It may take some time to complete; the best results will come with a patient and thorough story telling.

57

1. Describe fully something that you enjoy doing. This positive experience can come from leisure or work. In making this description, try to be as concrete as possible. For instance, suppose that you enjoy playing tennis. It is not enough to talk generally about the fun of playing tennis; instead, focus on a specific time that was particularly enjoyable. Perhaps you won a special game or learned a new strategy. Whatever the event is, describe it in as much detail as possible. Take a moment to list some key points from your description of the event. Include in this description how the event developed over time, what you were feeling and thinking, and why this particular event was so significant to you.

An Enjoyable Positive Event

2. Once you have completed the positive event, think of a parallel negative situation. Continuing with the above example, you would need to find an event in tennis that was not particularly enjoyable. It is important here to keep the negative situation within the same domain as the positive event; don't move too far afield. Of course, there may not be the same level of emotional involvement but usually you can find something that wasn't so enjoyable. Whatever the situation, list the key points of the situation in the space below.

59

A Parallel Negative Event That Wasn't Enjoyable

3. Now look at each of these situations and see if you can
    identify some of the underlying patterns. Some of the
    following questions might help you with this analysis.
    a. What are the relationships with the other people in
        each of these situations?

    b. What can you say about your personality by looking
        closely at the situations?

    c. Do these situations tell you anything about how you
        learn new information?

    d. What strengths or abilities can you identify?

e. Are there any special interests that you can identify?

f. What is it that really motivates you?

g. What rewards are important for you?

h. What is it that really frustrates you?

i. What do your frustrations tell you about what you consider to be important?

This analysis will hopefully provide you with some interesting insights into your basic life patterns. It may also be helpful at this point to get another person to go through this analysis with you. Sometimes a fresh perspective can be invaluable.

A further validation of your psychological DNA comes as you repeat this exercise in other areas of your life. If you initially used a leisure experience, change your focus and look at something from working life, in your home environment, as a volunteer, and so on. Sometimes you have to do several explorations in order to get the most out of the analysis.

The patterns that you identify may look something like the following:

- enjoy working with people / enjoy working alone
- enjoy challenges where everyone has to work together / frustrated when team work breaks down
- like finding ways to be successful, creative, innovative . . .
- like to solve problems
- want to make a difference / lose focus when others don't contribute to the team
- enjoy working with details / easily bogged down by details
- love to think about the big picture
- leading a group is energizing
- I'm happiest when I'm out in nature / sitting behind a desk all day is unbearable

Once you have identified some patterns, think about how these patterns might apply in new situations. Are there ways that these patterns can inform your problem solving and decision making? The patterns that you have identified will cut across individual and collective identities. Whatever their source, they tend to define your very being. For example, if you are thinking of making a career shift or accepting an employment opportunity, what type of situations bring you satisfaction and what might be some of the challenges that you will face? As you consider your own psychological DNA, what are the environments, both individual and collective, that will bring you joy and what individual and collective environments are most likely to rob you of joy?

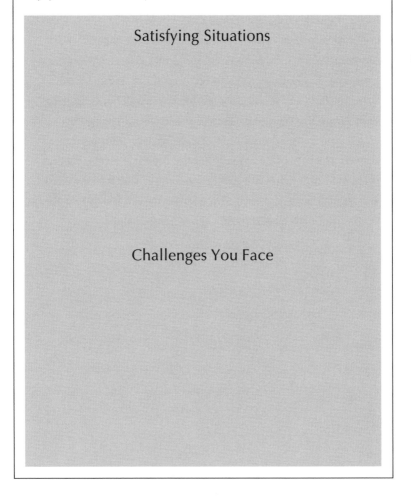

Satisfying Situations

Challenges You Face

Groups I Belong To

Another way to look at and for patterns is to examine the groups to which we belong. Within these groups, we often develop important aspects of our identity. The image I like to work with is one of a stone dropping into still water. The concentric circles that expand outward when a stone is dropped into a body of water can represent the impact we have in various communal groups. Those closest circles are the most fundamental relationships—perhaps family, peers, or working colleagues; and other circles of relationships move out from there. As an exercise, take some time to consider and describe your group involvements. Think broadly about the groups in which you are involved. Some of these groups undoubtedly operate at work, others in your leisure time; even within a family there are often many sub-groups operating. Just start by making a list of the various groups. Afterwards you can look more closely at what it means to belong to each of these groups.

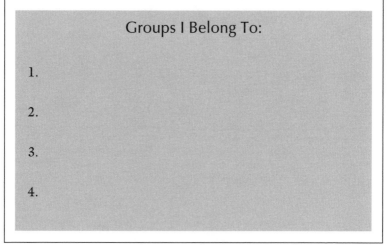

Groups I Belong To:

1.

2.

3.

4.

5.

6.

7.

8.

9.

10.

Although this exercise has a focus on groups, the questions posed help to focus attention on both individual and collective identities. Once you have listed your groups take time to think about your involvement in each situation. Here are some questions that you can use to help you with this reflection:

1. What benefits do you get from belonging to each group? Also, what are some of the disadvantages?

2. How did you come to be involved in each group? Did you choose for yourself, did someone else ask you to join in, or did you just "fall into" the group? How do you see your involvement continuing with the groups? Will you spend about the same amount of time with them, more time, or perhaps less time in the future?

66

3. What is the role that you play within the group? You may be an initiator, someone who keeps others happy, a visionary, planner, leader, supporter, etc. You may have more than one role depending on the situation. Also, you may not have chosen a particular role but find that others see you in a particular way. It might be helpful to think about how others might define your role in the group.

4. How satisfied are you with your involvement in each of the groups you have identified? Are your needs being met? Are there any groups that you would like to leave behind? Are there other groups that you would like to join?

5. Our immersion within groups helps to provide shape and direction to our lives. How do the groups that surround you impact your sense of identity? What values or beliefs are being reflected?

6. Finally, are there any new insights that you have gained? And probably the most important question, what actions might need to be taken to address any of the issues that you have identified? Take the time to develop a short action plan if this fits with your situation.

Action Plan

4

DIRECTION AND MAGNITUDE

... each new choice has consequences;
and depending on what we choose,
we can find ourselves in quite different places ...

... one of the signs of discernment and wisdom
is the ability to know
when to move forward and when to stand still ...

... as we increase the speed of our lives,
we are not just adding a few extra items of busyness;
the overall impact is compounded ...

A t this stage, if one can assume that a certain sense of balance has been established or restored with respect to the development of both an individual and collective identity, we can begin to consider some possibilities related to the movement of matter. There are certain key physical properties to consider that will help us along the way. First, in the physical world, the measurement of direction and magnitude as related to motion is determined by the use of what physics refers to as "vectors" and "scalars."

70

Vectors deal with the problems and possibilities related to both direction and magnitude—displacement, velocity, and acceleration. Displacement is the measurement of the pathways used to reach a particular goal. There are many ways to get to the same end point, and each pathway has its own measurement. Although it is commonly stated that the shortest distance between two points is a straight line, experience teaches us all very quickly that straight lines are not that common. While motion can be in a direct line, more often there is also movement back and forth and even sideways. These pathways have different shapes and different levels of efficiency in terms of reaching a goal, and so the displacement measurement also is variable.

DIRECTION AND MAGNITUDE

The velocity vector includes the measurement of both speed and direction. Wind is perhaps one of the most common phenomenon that we measure in terms of velocity. For example, we may hear weather reports describing the wind as travelling at 40 km per hour in a southwesterly direction (not all that uncommon where I grew up). Acceleration refers to the length of time that is required to attain a certain desired speed. Some people are more inclined towards quick starts; while others assume a slower and steadier pace of acceleration. The rate of acceleration will then influence the overall speed. The direction and speed in which you are travelling is of critical importance. If, as stated above, you are heading in a southwesterly direction then the directional coordinates will determine the nature of your journey as well as your end point. Of course, you might change direction midway but that is another matter that goes back to displacement.

In addition to vectors, there also are "scalars" such as distance, speed, mass, and temperature. These dimensions have a magnitude that can be measured (thus the term scalars) but they do not have direction. When we look at the movement of a particle, or particles in motion, we can measure how far it has gone, how fast it is moving, the heaviness of the object, and whether the particle in question is hot or cold (when temperature has the potential to impact magnitude). These measurements define the magnitude of an object but do not address its location or position, which is the work of vectors.

Psychological Vectors

Often used, but seldom recognized as such, are the psychological vectors and scalars that run as a parallel track to those of the physical world. As a measurement of the pathways used to reach our life / career goals, we need to take account of the level of **displacement** that is involved. If we frame this as a question, what are the decisions that we make in our lives and how do these decisions shape what is to follow? The well-known poem by Robert Frost "The Road Not Taken" highlights the mystery associated with the process of decision making.

72

The Road Not Taken

Two roads diverged in a yellow wood,
And sorry I could not travel both
And be one traveller, long I stood
And looked down one as far as I could
To where it bent in the undergrowth
Then took the other, as just as fair,

DIRECTION AND MAGNITUDE

And having perhaps the better claim,
Because it was grassy and wanted wear;
Though as for that the passing there
Had worn them really about the same,
And both that morning equally lay
In leaves no step had trodden blank.
Oh, I kept the first for another day!
Yet knowing how way leads on to way,
I doubted if I should ever come back.
I shall do this with a sigh
Somewhere ages and ages hence;
Two roads diverged in a wood, and I
Took the one less travelled by
And that has made all the difference!

As path leads on to path, so too we make choices about where and how to go on. Each new choice has consequences; and depending on what we choose, we can find ourselves in quite different places along the way. The concept of displacement helps to capture this notion of different pathways, of forward, sideways, and sometimes even backward movement, and inevitably the end point. We have to take account of the impact of the journey itself on the end destination. Some find their destination early on, others do a lot more searching, and, sadly, there are

those who become completely lost along the way. Robert
Frost reminds us that some choices fundamentally change
our lives.

We need to consider this issue of choice at two
different levels. At certain times we can be almost paralyzed
by the enormity of the choices we are making. But there
are also times when the choices do not have the same level
of long-term impact. It is important to make this

distinction. As someone who has worked with many young
people on the issue of career choice, I am always struck by
the way in which decisions at the end of high school often
are framed in a false curtain of finality. Will the young
person choose college or work as a direction? If school is
the direction, what field of study or training will be
pursued? Certainly decisions have to be made, but what is
frequently forgotten is that there are many futures,
opportunities for change "as way leads on to way." The
education process itself gives witness to velocity and
acceleration. Some finish with a flourish; while others take
a few more years. The end point may be similar, but there
are different pathways that will require different lengths of
time and varying degrees of focus. The same can be said for
many other personal and career choices.

There are also those decisions that do fundamentally
change our lives, the decisions we make that lead to

dramatically different life experiences. The significance of these life choices rest in their power to simultaneously touch more than one dimension of our life. Traumas, such as unexpected illness, an accident, or death, fit into this category. Within some cultures various vows or covenants have great power over the different dimensions of our lives. Perhaps there are a few who have won lotteries or other prizes that have opened doors never before thought possible. My own choice as a young adult to live within a Christian worldview has provided a significant focus in all dimensions. As I struggled with this choice at many different levels—intellectually, emotionally, and socially, I sought out the counsel of teachers and philosophers as well as those who I knew cared deeply for me as a person. Ultimately, it was a single personal step of faith, a step that I have taken and re-taken on a daily basis. It is the nature of spirituality that such decisions have the power to change many aspects of a life and to continue to shape and direct the pathways that are ahead.

The **velocity** and **acceleration** vectors touch upon our speed and direction as we make choices. Sometimes we can be moving at a rapid pace but moving in a completely wrong direction. Rather than getting closer to the goal, we are in fact moving further away. Certainly this type of behavior is common in a world where the rules are rapidly changing. Take for example the person who is mass-producing resumes in the hope that someone "out there" will take an interest. While this activity may create a lot of movement, it may not be the most effective job search strategy.

In addition to velocity and acceleration, it is also helpful to focus on the regulation of speed. There are times when it is productive to move quickly and take advantage of opportunities. There are also times when we need to slow down and proceed with caution. To be able to regulate "velocity," both our desired speed and the pace of acceleration is undoubtedly a useful life skill. One of the signs of discernment and wisdom in this area is the ability to know when to move forward and when to stand still. Acquiring this skill requires clarity of purpose and some moments of quiet reflection. As I watch people scurry about with cell phones and lap top computers, I wonder how much is actually being accomplished. For many people, the busyness creates a sense of motion without necessarily having any real sense of direction. Even though people are working hard, they are moving further away from any form of life and career satisfaction. Activity without focus creates an imbalance and does not contribute to our overall well-being.

However, there are times when we can move ahead enthusiastically and with full confidence in our actions. At such times, there is a sense of "flow" (Csikszentmihalyi, 1990). On such occasions, the best rest is full involvement. Passion and commitment carry the individual into these activities; life is lived wholeheartedly and fully. Love has this kind of power, this kind of experience and goal. But lest we digress, as can so easily be done when speaking of love, let us return to the matter at hand.

77

Scalars: Distance, Speed, Mass, Temperature

Distance

The issue of short- and long-term goals relates directly to the measurement of **distance**. If we let our goals become too distant, we lose our point of reference and start to drift. The point of short-term goals is to help us break the long journey into manageable parts. Achieving short-term goals allows us to infuse celebration and success into our journey. The journey is as important as the destination or goal.

I spend a considerable amount of time on my bicycle; and during this time, I have the opportunity to think about goals and their ability to keep our paths straight and true. One of the roads that follow the river I often cycle beside has many curves and bends. Sometimes, as I ride, I will look at the thin white line along the edge of this road and try to keep my bicycle tires on the line. At times, I will try to maintain a vigorous pace while looking down at the white line. At other times, I focus on a spot further down the road and keep my eyes fixed on the future goal while maintaining the same vigorous pace. My son tries the same activity; perhaps all bikers do at some point along the way. The result is always the same. The wobble is reduced considerably when we look further up the road. If my head is too focused on the ground directly in front of me, the "wobble effect" dramatically increases. As I reflect on this little experiment with cycling the white line, I find many parallels to the way in which we live our lives. If we are too focused on the details, we lose the way and start to spend an inordinate amount of time on non-essentials. The opposite is also true: if our goals are too distant, they are not helpful and we flounder. Again, we come back to the issue of balance.

Speed

The second scalar, **speed**, certainly plays an important role in defining the nature of motion. An interesting fact associated with speed is that the impact of moving is not something that progresses in a straight line. Rather, impact is assessed using the square of a number (Bodanis, 2000). Suppose, for example, that you were driving a car at 20 kilometers per hour and the car stopped suddenly. You can measure the skid marks to measure impact. Now, increase the speed to 80 kilometers per hour and take similar measurements after stopping suddenly. In a straight progression, the skid mark at the faster speed would be four times as long. In reality, the impact is 4 times 4 or 16 times what it is at the lower speed. As a metaphor, we can see in our own lives that as we increase the speed of our lives, we are not just adding a few extra items of busyness. The overall impact is compounded and so too, when we want to slow down, it takes much longer to come to that place of rest. Complete rest for many is an illusion until we reach the point where one extra thing has pushed us over the edge, and rest comes in the form of recovery.

Of course, speed itself is not the problem; it is rather a matter of moving at safe levels. Without any speed, inertia sets in and there is the tendency to stay at rest until there is

79

some infusion of energy into the system. With too much speed, there is loss of control and another set of problems emerges. Somewhere between these two extremes exists action that is vigorous but also controlled.

The value of controlled speed is something that anyone who has tried to drive through a snowdrift on a rural road can appreciate. As a young man growing up in the Canadian prairies, I would find myself at times on a road blocked because of drifting snow. Turning back was not an option since one could not tell where the road ended and the ditches began. In most instances, it was a matter of "taking a run" at the snow barrier. Of course, there were a few occasions when I misjudged the length and depth of the snow and had to be pulled from the snow bank by a kind farmer. In most situations, however, I was able to "power" through the barrier and move forward. Sometimes we need to have more encouragement to "power" through the barriers that confront us, particularly through those barriers that are of our own making. Sometimes we can lend a hand to others who haven't been so successful.

I experienced a significant internal barrier (a deep snow requiring not just power but also a metaphoric shovel and persistent patient effort) at one point in my life. I encountered a difficult situation in a training group that I was leading. For some reason, this event played on my mind and started to affect my performance in other situations. I began to be anxious whenever I was going to speak to a new group and this anxiety grew to the point of full-blown panic attacks. For someone who earned his living speaking to groups of people this was a catastrophic situation. I was able to function adequately after an initial introductory period, but the beginning phase was a nightmare. My voice would crack and my breathing became uneven. The downward spiral was rapid. From a three-dimensional perspective, I felt my life was over. The only thing that kept me going was the depth of support from family members and a few close friends and the depth of my spiritual beliefs. Most people had no idea about what I was going through. At one point, I felt the bottom and made a decision to keep on trying to speak whatever the consequences. I struggled to regain my composure and used every aid that I could. I found it helpful to pray, to arrive early, to be well prepared, to have a glass of water close at hand. I also found ways of guiding the conversation so that I could give myself breaks if they were needed. These simple guidelines seemed to help. Lastly, I pushed myself to carry on. Even when it would have been easy to turn down a speaking engagement, I persisted. The anxiety is still with me but now it has been reduced to a mere whisper. At one level I am thankful for this experience since it has helped me to appreciate the power of anxiety.

Temperature

Applying scalars to the above scenario, I think it would be fair to say that I lost **speed** and changed my internal **temperature** through emotional turmoil. I certainly lost confidence and wanted to withdraw from the world (a new direction—in this sense a shift in displacement). The anxiety seemed to grow by leaps and bounds and threatened to run through all aspects of my life. I felt "ice" in my veins whenever I faced a new situation where I would meet people. And yet I somehow persisted and found within myself (with support) the capacity to eventually push back the anxiety that threatened to overwhelm me. (Note: This is the first time that I have written openly about this affliction. I hope that through these words others will gain hope and find the courage to struggle on whatever the circumstances.)

Mass

The final scalar addresses the issue of **mass**. It is difficult to undertake any journey when you are burdened with excess mass or bulk. This bulk can be physical (as I am prone to experience), psychological, emotional, or even spiritual. Whatever the situation, excess mass acts like an anchor. In the context of the earlier discussion on busyness, excess busyness creates extra "width" and impedes our movement forward. Certainly, with extra mass, it can be difficult to generate the speed we might need. It is also more difficult to manoeuvre bulky loads and to maintain balance when the terrain is uneven or sloped. There also are health concerns associated with the accumulation of mass. Even if we are able to keep going, our physical system and our psyche, depending on what we are carrying, is placed under increased stress; this stress may be lead to unexpected short- or long-term consequences. The best travellers travel light.

Overcoming Roadblocks on the Journey

This section on direction and measurement draws heavily on the metaphor of the journey. There are many elements associated with moving along life's pathways. At times there are impediments along the way, there are difficult choices to be made; there are times when we need to gather strength and times when we need to find a new way. There are also times when everything seems to go smoothly, when we feel strong and the choices seem clear.

84

As you think about your present position, there may be some issues that you are trying to resolve. Rather than trying to do everything at once, try to limit your focus to one of the challenges you are facing. What are some of the impediments or roadblocks in front of you? Take the time to write down an issue you are facing and the accompanying roadblocks.

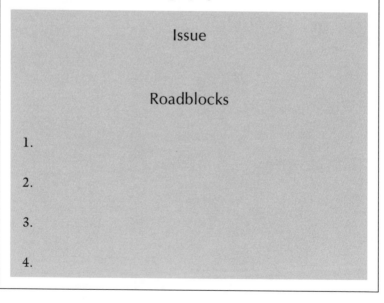

Issue

Roadblocks

1.

2.

3.

4.

Overcoming roadblocks is not easy and to be successful, you need to be aware of all of your personal resources. It is very easy to "sell yourself short." To ensure that you have a full inventory of your personal resources, you will find it helpful to look back at other challenges that you have faced in the past. What were those situations and how did you handle them? Look at several examples and identify some of your ways of coping with challenges (i.e., personal qualities, support received, skills applied, spiritual resources).

1. A Previous Challenge

How I Successfully Coped With This Challenge

2. A Previous Challenge

How I Successfully Coped With This Challenge

3. A Previous Challenge

How I Successfully Coped With This Challenge

Can you identify any common coping patterns? How might you apply some of these strengths to your current situation? Brainstorm some possibilities.

For job seekers, the following roadmap has been used as part of the Starting Points program for youth (Borgen & Amundson, 1996). You will note that the roadmap has both roadblocks where you may encounter problems or barriers and stopovers where personal resources may be enhanced.

DIRECTION AND MAGNITUDE

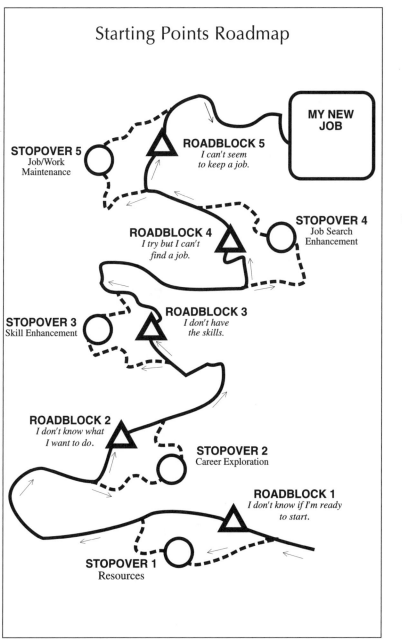

87

You can use the image of a roadmap to think about any type of problem that you might be facing. Make a roadmap of the journey you are contemplating, and on this roadmap place the roadblocks and also the stopovers / resources you might use to overcome each of the roadblocks.

My Journey's Roadmap

Look carefully at the roadmap you have created. What will you need to get started? Develop an action plan.

Action Plan

5

QUANTUM
THINKING

*... our paradigm has shifted away from stability, order,
uniformity, and equilibrium towards a new order
of instability, disorder, disequilibrium, and non-linear
relationships where small inputs can trigger major effects ...*

*... quantum thinking contains within it
a readiness to accept contradictions and paradoxes
and an ability to view events from multiple perspectives ...*

*... we need to find ways to 'still our minds' in the midst of chaos
and to find new ways of making sense of our lives ...*

The general rules of motion as outlined by Isaac Newton changed for scientists when they increased the speed at which objects moved to speeds approaching the speed of light (Tipler, 1991). Suddenly a new world opened up to them (sometimes called quantum mechanics or wave mechanics). Using quantum physics, scientists came to realize that although atoms are separate entities, it was impossible to measure them exactly or to predict with absolute precision what they would do. This lack of precision flew in the face of traditional science and suggested that no matter how careful the measurement, there would always be some element of error. This paradigm shift moved away from stability, order, uniformity, and equilibrium and suggested a new order of instability, disorder, disequilibrium, and non-linear relationships where small inputs could trigger major effects. In coming to terms with this new reality, scientists had to open themselves up to a universe that included both stable and more chaotic systems.

Ilya Prigogine, a scientist who won the Nobel Prize in 1977, and his colleague Isabelle Stengers (1984) helped lay a foundation for a new science of chaos and complexity.

They make the suggestion that even under the most chaotic conditions there seems to be a self-organizing principle that helps systems to develop higher levels of order or organization. They illustrate how order can be found in chaos and how instability can be the starting point for transformation. Their theory also describes a change process that is heavily influenced by what might be described as relatively minor events.

Many of these quantum ideas fit with what is occurring within the social and psychological realms. There was a point in time when many behavioral scientists felt that they could predict and control human behavior if they just had enough information. However, there has been a shift in orientation. Quantum thinking is part of a post-modern lifestyle. Current theories, such as constructivism, recognize the unique ways in which people create meaning in their life. With this view, there is considerable room for uncertainty and higher-order complexity. Rather than run from this complexity and uncertainty, we need to move forward and embrace the paradoxes that confront us.

Applying quantum principles to our lives provides some interesting challenges. There is considerable evidence to suggest that we live in a time of rapid social and economic change. In our "fast-paced" world many of the traditional rules for working and personal life no longer seem to apply.

The high "speed" of change has shattered many traditional assumptions, and we are forced to incorporate greater uncertainty and complexity into our conceptions of the world. It is within this context that we need to consider how to apply quantum thinking to our everyday lives. An example from working life is the faith that many people place in the organization. In the past, private and public organizations created an image of security and paternalistic care. That image has been tarnished for some and shattered for others. People are realizing that it is time to find or create a new foundation for their lives. Economic turmoil and a marketplace redefined through technology and globalization (Herr, 1999) touches everyone. With new economic structures, the psychological contract between workers and employers has shifted. Many firms have a flatter organizational structure, more emphasis on productivity, less job security, and often higher levels of stress and burnout (Feller, 1995). For some people the change in structure is a serious problem; for others it represents new opportunities and more freedom to direct their own career development efforts (Arthur, Inkson, & Pringle, 1999; Lewin & Rigine, 2000). Whatever the perspective, people of all ages are increasingly asking questions about work life as they prepare for new economic realities.

For many people, family and friends are becoming more central along with a renewed spirituality. Within this effort for renewal, organizational life is still important, but it is viewed from a more realistic perspective. Rather than a full-scale commitment to the organization, there is connection to certain projects and people within the organization and the acknowledgement that the responsibility for career development ultimately falls on the shoulders of the individual.

95

Quantum thinking also influences the goals that we set for ourselves. Traditionally people learned to set goals and move towards them more or less in a straight line. But what if the goals start changing and the pathways toward them become circular or dead ends? What if we decide the goal is no longer desirable? In a high-speed world, what if our goal "disappears" or ceases to exist due to changes beyond our control? Does goal setting even make sense in a context of fast-paced change? Goals are obviously important but now need to be held with an open hand. We need to be prepared to make adjustments along the way, even to discard goals and to establish new ones that are more consistent with present circumstances. In some situations, all we can do is position ourselves for potential new opportunities. Our choices always reflect certain contextual limits. We avoid being pushed and pulled by external needs, desires, and demands, knowing that when external pressures take control, personal influence is lost and we are forced into the more passive role of acceptance or compliance. Passively, we are left with only minimal conscious choice and decision making power.

Contextually, we live with shifting social, economic, and political orders. Perhaps talk of politics and economics seems far removed from where we live and plan a life; the reality is that we can be impacted at a very personal level by these global affairs. Socially, we confront complex choices and changing definitions related to relationships, sexuality, deviancy, crime, health, drugs, and life and death itself.

This new reality is euphoria for some, but we also need to recognize that many unskilled and disadvantaged people are left behind. It is not a uniform upwardly mobile spiral. Many people find themselves struggling to survive in the new economy. This dual economic track is widening at an alarming pace. Reid (1996), in a report of economic trends, points to the fact that in 1972 the average corporate executive made 44 times as much as the average corporate worker. By 1992 the gap had widened to a stunning 222 to 1. The impact of this disparity of wealth distribution continues to be felt at many different levels. Certainly education and health care standards have been lowered; this brings us again to complex social choices.

Politically, there is little doubt that we are in the midst of profound change. The collapse of communism in the Soviet Union, the formation of new countries, terrorism— all of this and more threatens to overwhelm us. Within such a social, economic, and political shifting of the proverbial sands of time, the challenge is to embrace flexibility and to make the necessary adjustments along the way.

With an increasing number of choices, and increasing uncertainty about those choices, we need to find ways to "still our minds" in the midst of chaos and to find new ways of staying in the "flow" and of continuing to make sense of our lives. The best decisions, the decisions that will see us through, are not made from a "hurry up" mode but rather when we have attained a more reflective inner space.

This "stilling of the mind" does not necessarily mean that we arrive at a state of inertia. Often we have to conduct our assessment at the same time as we are moving forward. The payoff for taking steps in the midst of uncertain goals is that when we are in motion, we are concerned primarily with direction and don't have to exert additional energy to initiate movement. The danger with uncertainty and complexity is that people will stop moving (forward or sideways) and then become paralyzed by indecision. Another principle of physics is that it takes

97

considerably more energy to get matter up to a desired speed after a state of inertia has been attained.

Gelatt (1989) has used the term "positive uncertainty" to refer to this new constellation of skills and attitudes that incorporate quantum thinking. He puts together two seemingly contradictory terms, a shift from "either-or" thinking to "both-and" thinking. We need to be positive and fully engaged in our actions and, at the same time, be ready to shift focus when the context changes. This focus on "both-and" thinking flows through many different career and life issues. For example, I have been asked on many occasions whether it is best to be a career generalist or a specialist. The answer today is that you need both; you need to have a good solid general education and you also need to have special skills that set you apart from others. This perspective on life suggests a new more open attitude toward learning and a creative crafting of career (Poehnell & Amundson, 2002).

Motion with uncertainty does not mean random action. Mitchell, Levin, and Krumboltz (1999) have an interesting perspective on how some people maintain a high state of readiness even when they appear to be standing still. Their studies have led them to examine the influence of unexpected or chance events in career planning. What they discovered was that when you really examine these "chance" events in detail, it becomes clear that there was often more going on than was immediately obvious. I have started to apply this process to my own work and in a recent seminar situation asked people to think about their own career paths and the role of chance or luck in that scenario. I remember one person in particular who described his entry into the counselling profession as a "fluke." He had tried different jobs and on the last one was downsized and received a severance package. With the money he decided to go back to school and, by chance, met someone who suggested the counselling program. When I explored this scenario in more detail, some additional information came out. He actually voluntarily decided to take the severance package because he didn't like his job and was looking for something else. Also, he didn't just run into someone who suggested counselling but rather actively sought out some people for career discussions. When he decided to pursue the counselling program, he was too late to submit his application. Despite this setback he met with people and left his application. A space opened up in the program shortly thereafter and he was admitted. Mitchell, Levin, and Krumboltz (1999, p. 118) describe some of the skills and attitudes that accompany some of these chance events as follows:

1. **Curiosity:** exploring new learning opportunities.
2. **Persistence:** exerting effort despite setbacks.
3. **Flexibility:** changing attitudes and circumstances.
4. **Optimism:** viewing new opportunities as possible and attainable.
5. **Risk Taking:** taking action in the face of uncertain outcomes.

They suggest that people who have adopted this orientation "are willing to change plans, take risks, work hard to overcome obstacles, and be actively engaged in pursuing their interests" (p. 120). In the story just told, there is little doubt that many of these skills and attitudes were present. The person left his job with no clear career future (risk taking); he was generally optimistic about the future; he wanted to try something different (curiosity); and in the face of missed deadlines, he persisted and remained optimistic and flexible.

According to two other authors, Guindon and Hanna (2002), the understanding of "chance" events is not always so easy to understand. They make the point that there are times when this self-organizing function seems to defy rational explanation. For many people this is a point where the spiritual dimension becomes an important tool for understanding. Certainly in my own life I can look back on the way in which many events have unfolded and feel that the hand of God was at work. Often these patterns only become evident from a retrospective perspective.

The focus on quantum thinking contains within it a readiness to accept contradictions and paradoxes. Charles Handy (1994) calls our current age the Age of Paradox. Similar to other authors, he makes the case that we need to accept the reality of mystery and uncertainty and learn effective action strategies within this context. One of the points that I find particularly compelling is his use of the "S" curve. Handy suggests that in many ways our pathways reflect a series of "S" curves rather than straight lines. We start off in a certain direction, then need to make certain adjustments (rapid learning), and finally level off on a new pathway. There is growth and development in these changes; but if we hang on too long, the end of the "S" starts to dip and we get a rapid drop. In many ways, it reminds me of my experiences in the stock market. In the beginning there were the challenges of finding potential winners. At times, I would be successful and watch my stock soar. Then there would be the inevitable decline. Unfortunately, I would still be hanging onto my stock as it dropped off the board. Handy points out that the most difficult decisions involve knowing when to get off the "S" curve. You can get off too early and miss some great upward movement, or you can hang on too long and watch all your gains evaporate. Knowing when to make changes is really the true "art" of career development.

The starting point for change requires some new involvement and perspectives. In this regard, I am reminded of a recent experience while cycling with a colleague. As we rode, we saw a car with two people in it that was stuck in a field of sand. The driver, intent on getting out, continued to push the gas pedal to the floor.

Smoke was coming from the car, and sand was flying as the wheels sunk deeper. A lot of energy was being used but little was accomplished. In the car were two retired women who had decided to take their car off the road to do a few spins in the sand (perhaps to be young once more). Unfortunately they were now hopelessly stuck. The response to their dilemma was similar to many other responses to problems that we often face. We get "stuck" and, in our frenzy to get out, we use methods (like pushing on the accelerator) that are no longer effective. In fact, by using these methods, we usually make the situation worse. What needs to be done? Our first step was to get the women out of the car to look at the situation from a new perspective. After some collaborative discussion, we developed a plan. We found a board and started to dig out the back tires (a new strategy!). They then got back in the car and we started to push from the front of the vehicle.

Eventually a tire caught the wood so there was some traction and slowly (part of the strategy was to not use full power) the car moved out of the hole in the sand. The story ended happily and we continued on our bike ride. Sometimes the best strategy is simply to stop what we are doing and take some time to look at our situation from a fresh perspective. We can do this through our own efforts but also may benefit from involving others in the struggles we face.

Quantum thinking has at its core the ability to view events from multiple perspectives. Rather than one particular viewpoint, a shift in perspectives offers new insight. Each shift in perspective provides more understanding. In some ways it is like "flying with eagles." In our area of the country there are many bald eagles, and I love watching them soar on the wind. As they soar with circular motions of an increasing size, their position gradually shifts so that over a period of time they are in a completely new place with a new view, a new perspective. Perhaps we need to let ourselves soar like the eagles and take up the challenge of multiple perspectives.

This image of flying with eagles is meant to capture the need to obtain separation or distance from the problems we are facing. This separation can be experienced in many ways. It can be a process where emotional and conceptual separation is realized by finding a different lens to examine the problem. Finding this new lens may involve stepping out from the frantic pace of life, seeking advice from others, acquiring some new information, challenging oneself to look at a situation from a new point of view, letting time pass and letting the experience reorganize itself into a new configuration, or simply seeking physical separation from a problem. The next section will examine in more detail some of these methods.

Applying Quantum Thinking in Our Lives

Quantum Theory points toward the importance of broadening perspectives and challenging conventional thinking. Rather than narrowing our categories, it is important that we expand our viewpoints and be willing to suspend judgment, even in the face of contradictory information. One of the most basic activities within this framework is "dreaming" possibilities (not just a nighttime activity). When you are dreaming, you can suspend judgment and ideas flow freely. It takes time and a real willingness to be open. Often we are in too much of a hurry to allow ourselves the freedom to be "still" and just sit back and listen to the small voice within us as we dream possibilities. I should also add here that it is a real discipline to learn to be "still." If you have been going at breakneck speed and living within a somewhat chaotic situation, it takes awhile for the mind to slow down. Think about past vacations that you have taken. Often it takes a day or two before you really start acting like you are on vacation. The same applies to "stilling" our minds. We need to allow sufficient time for the noise to disappear. It is only within the stillness that conditions will be right for growing new ideas.

In my life I have found peace and quiet in various activities. When my children were younger, I used to enjoy washing supper dishes after a day's work. During this somewhat mindless activity, my mind would drift through my day or I would begin to dream new ideas. Now that technology has taken over my dishwashing, the same thing happens on my bicycle. I look at nature and find inspiration. My mind wanders and new thoughts emerge. There are many ways to find quiet moments. For most of us, the most difficult thing is just to stop and be still (without falling asleep). As I have tried to be still, I have found that initially my mind is whirring and I am listening to every small sound, perhaps fighting the very act of being quiet. It is only through persistence that I finally can break through the barriers between busyness and active stillness.

In our busy world, it is an art to create quiet space inside and outside of our selves.

Within the quiet spaces, we are better able to identify and separate inner voices that are positive and life giving from those that are negative and overly critical. As I have listened to my own inner voices, I hear the following messages:

Negative messages

1. Expectations of others, for example, "in this situation I should always...."
2. Evaluating the actions of others, for example, "this can't be real, what are they up to."
3. Before attempting new actions, for example, "I'll never be able to do that, it didn't work last time."
4. A challenging situation, for example, "this is too hard, I give up."
5. Evaluating success, for example, "I was just lucky, watch out for next time."
6. Evaluating failure, for example, "that's the way it is, I better not try again."
7. Everything is going well, for example, "this won't last, it will soon fall apart."

Positive Messages

1. Give freely to others and don't look for immediate rewards.
2. Be true to yourself.
3. Treat others fairly and in ways that you would like to be treated.
4. Help out those that are most in need.
5. Keep trying.
6. You can figure things out.
7. Speak the truth.

Finding the time and the quiet space to reflect on these inner voices is an activity that is well worth the time and effort. Most of the critical messages lose their power under any form of careful examination. Buried in our minds, they gain power by casting shadows over our behaviour.

Messages

Identify some of the common critical voices that have found a way into your life. Chapter Seven addresses some of the methods for challenging negative messages.

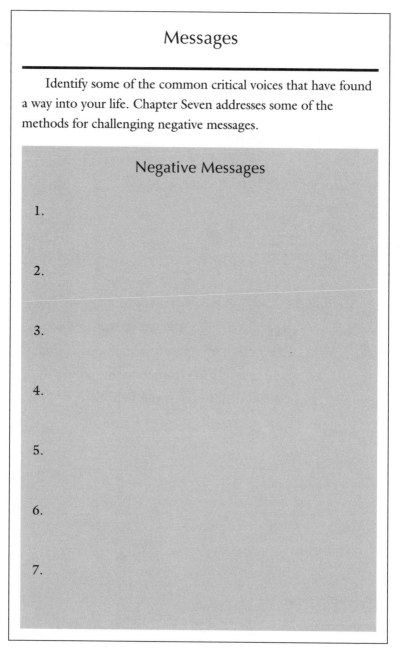

Negative Messages

1.

2.

3.

4.

5.

6.

7.

Identify some of the positive and affirming voices that have found a way into your life.

Positive Messages

1.

2.

3.

4.

5.

6.

7.

"Chance" Events

Another activity, based the work of Mitchell, Levin, and Krumboltz (1999) as described earlier in this chapter, confronts passivity and focuses on the way in which we interpret events. The emphasis here is upon perceived "chance" events in work or personal life. To begin the activity take a moment to list some of the chance events that you have observed in your life.

"Chance" Events

1.

2.

3.

4.

5.

Now, look more closely at these events. Were they "purely chance"? Perhaps there is more happening in these events than just chance. Often when positive things happen, we acknowledge the chance elements but don't see how we also contributed to what happened. How did any of the following qualities play a part in your response to the chance events you listed above?

QUANTUM THINKING

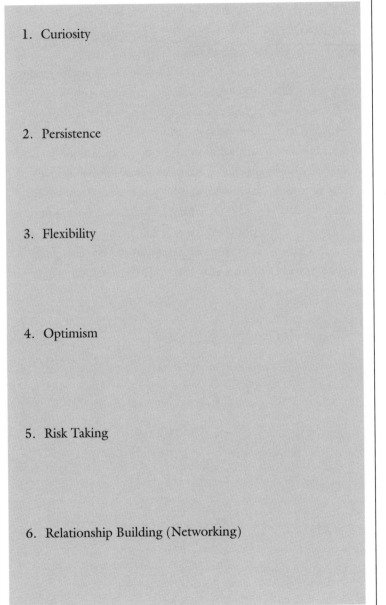

1. Curiosity

2. Persistence

3. Flexibility

4. Optimism

5. Risk Taking

6. Relationship Building (Networking)

These six elements often are associated with many so-called chance occurrences. It is helpful to take ownership of our part in these events, to seek ways to make "chance" a part of our planning. People who seek and take advantage of unexpected opportunities are those who employ curiosity, persistence, flexibility, optimism, and risk taking in their everyday lives.

Quantum thinking draws attention to the extent to which we shut out other options when we make decisions. I think about some of the times in which I have had various possibilities to weigh. Sometimes it feels so good to just make a decision and develop an action plan. The natural inclination at this point is to push all the other options to the side and to move forward. While this may work in some situations, in our fast changing world we need to remain alert and ready to take advantage of new opportunities.

6

ENERGY

TRANSFER

*... there are times when we give more energy
and other times when we benefit from the energy
that is returned to us from others ...*

*... the dilemma is how to share energy
and at the same time ensure
that there is not an overall decline in energy
for the person offering help ...*

*... regeneration of energy often requires a step backward
(a backswing) before one is in a position to move forward ...*

T he First Law of Thermodynamics can be stated as follows: "The sum of the heat added and the work done on a system equals the change in the internal energy of the system" (Tipler, 1991, p. 536). At its most basic level, this means that when a hot object is in contact with a cool object, there is an internal energy transfer (heat) from the warm object to the cooler object. The electrons connected to the atoms of warmer objects move quickly; and when they collide with cooler objects (electrons moving slower), energy is transferred and a new equilibrium is established with a moderated temperature. In this new state, the temperature of the hot object is reduced and the temperature of the cool object is increased.

In ordinary conversation, energy metaphors are used frequently to describe the movement of energy in interpersonal relationships (i.e., spark, flow, vibes). Also, in describing working life, people refer to being burned out (no energy flow) or to having their energy circuits overloaded. It seems that this idea of energy transfer can be applied to many situations. Whenever people apply themselves to a task, there is an expenditure of energy. The same can be said for relationships and the connections we form with others. Energy flow is not always in one direction. Like a rechargeable battery, there are times when we give more energy and other times when we benefit from the energy that is returned to us from others. In this chapter, I will be addressing both how energy flow can be helpful to us and also how it presents some real challenges, particularly at times when we lose too much energy.

Heat transfer is part of normal working and personal life. We expect to be in situations where we offer warmth (energy) to others and receive warmth in turn. Take for example the person working as an employment counsellor. Clients who are having difficulty can be characterized as "having a lower than desired temperature." They have run out of ideas for solving their problems and need to rebuild self confidence. They need an infusion of energy to get them moving again. The counsellor is in a position to expend energy by listening to problems and by sharing new ideas and insights. The satisfaction of helping someone make a positive change provides some energy back to the counsellor. There also are other activities such as professional development workshops, dialogue with colleagues, retreats, and time away with supportive folk that hopefully help to rebuild energy resources. Such activities are part of normal working activities and as such also require energy; but not only can they use energy, they can also allow energy to be restored.

Natural Warmth

Some people seem to be naturally warm. They are sensitive and empathic and find themselves more closely connected to other people and their environment. All work situations depend on harmony and teamwork. People who are able to easily connect with colleagues, managers, and clients are an invaluable resource within any company. There also are some professions that depend heavily on this type of warmth (i.e., social work, teaching, human resources, counselling).

There are ways for people to improve their level of warmth. While there may be some underlying biological factors, there also are ways that people can better equip themselves. One way to build warmth is to connect with a greater range of people and situations. Sometimes our lives are just too narrow. By meeting and listening to people with different ideas and values, we extend our warmth and general range of empathic behavior. This may be accomplished through travel, but we can also take the initiative to connect more broadly in our own community. Sometimes we get trapped with the same set of friends and develop a narrow band of contacts. Taking the initiative to meet different groups of people within our own communities can improve our understanding of others and thus build warmth. Another building block for warmth is influenced by the extent to which we relate to our world from a position of power. From positions of power, it is very difficult to perceive accurately what is happening around us. I have always been fascinated by the stories of "powerful leaders" who develop their abilities to understand and work with people. It seems that the only way to develop this special sense of understanding and warmth is to live among the people without any form of pretense. In the stories, kings take off their robes and live for a time with ordinary people. People in power positions remember the lessons they learned before they acquired wealth and influence. Some important lessons in life are learned when people have to focus on the needs of others.

Of course, warmth has its limits and, as was mentioned earlier, may contribute to burnout. Frost and Robinson (1999) describe the roles of some people in organizations as "toxic handlers." Through their natural empathy (warmth), they listen to the problems of others and help to reduce "toxicity" in the work environment. This type of action is invaluable to the organization and to the people involved; it also carries personal risk. The same can be said for people who work in the helping professions. In undertaking this role, one needs to be able to handle the natural depletion of energy. The dilemma is how to share energy and at the same time ensure that there is not an overall decline in energy for the person offering help.

Burnout

Increasingly, people work in situations where the demands far outstrip any energy replenishment possibilities (Amundson, Borgen, Ehrlebach, & Jordan, in press). Cutbacks and downsizing have reduced the number of workers in many industries and at the same time the work has become more complex. The end result is a constant pressure for more energy. The pressure does not end with the normal workday; many work extra hours to keep up with the demands. Also, the complexity of working life seems to be ever increasing. Workers are often given new responsibilities with little training or supervision. The result is a growing gap between the needs in the workplace and the ability of people to meet those needs. People are forced to run ever faster just to stay in the same place as they try to keep up with the escalating demands. From a heat transfer perspective, there is just too little heat (energy) to meet the demand. Like a water heater that is taxed to the

limit (I was raised in a large family), there comes a time
when the heat source is exhausted and the water just runs
cold.

The end result of this type of energy differential is
burnout. As people try to push themselves to meet
external demands, they begin to sacrifice their own well-
being. Increasingly, I meet people who suffer from burnout
and others who seem to be on a similar path. When I
inquire about the employees who are most susceptible to
burnout, the answer is always the same. It is the "best"
employees that seem to be most at risk, workers that take
to heart the needs of people and the organization and,
despite their hard work and good intent, are unable to
maintain the frantic pace.

This energy drain is not limited to working life.
Problems in our personal lives also require great
expenditures of energy. Hobson, Delunas, and Kesic
(2001) conducted a national U.S. study of stressful events.
In their survey, respondents were asked to rate the
perceived stressfulness of 51 distinct life events. None of
the ten most stressful life events were specifically work
related (i.e., death and dying, life threatening illness,
divorce, institutional detention, and so on). Despite the
personal nature of these concerns, it is not hard to imagine
how these events affect every aspect of our lives.

Managing Energy Flow

In light of the high demand for energy flow, it is important that we learn how to respond to needs in a balanced fashion. Without some form of control, there is a natural tendency to overextend and wind up in a burnout situation. There are various ways to develop control. One option is to ensure that energy is regenerated on a continuous basis. If someone is in an energy-draining role without replenishment, we know that they run the risk of burnout. So, a starting point is to ensure that time is allocated to be away from the situation, time to focus on self-care. In the workplace, this may be as simple as ensuring that people take lunch breaks away from the office, away from any demands that do not restore balance. At another level, there is value in taking designated holidays as an extended time to shift the focus from regular work projects. People who assume energy draining roles need to ensure that they have some way of taking breaks and rebuilding energy reserves. This form of energy buildup usually takes us back to earlier considerations of a balanced life where time and energy are devoted to a wide range of activities.

From another angle, one way to limit the drain of energy is to place some restrictions (boundaries) on contact time. Perhaps it is not necessary to respond continually to the stated needs of others. I am thinking here of situations where someone might be in a caregiver role and drained by constant requests for help. Rather than responding in a continuous energy draining fashion, it might be possible to encourage the person requesting help to draw energy from their own resources. From this perspective the caregiver acts more as a catalyst and less as an ongoing energy source. The person seeking help is not viewed as totally dependent or helpless. Rather, each person is viewed as having internal resources that just need to be ignited, much like lighting a pilot light. In the long run this perspective reduces dependence, people who receive help learn to regenerate their own energy and, through this process, begin to help not only themselves but also others.

123

The need to set boundaries around contact time is something that touches our lives at many different points. As the information age unfolds, we find ourselves having new opportunities for communication but also facing new challenges. A good example is e-mail. As someone who connects with people in many different countries, I have found e-mail to be an invaluable resource. At the same time, I am becoming increasingly aware of the addictive nature of this form of communication. It is so easy to become enslaved to the machine, to keep checking for messages even when other work needs to be done. Again, it is a matter of finding the right balance. For myself, that means focusing on my other work and reminding myself that I don't have to immediately respond to every e-mail message that comes my way.

Another way to manage energy flow is to recognize that energy transfer does not necessarily have to come solely from one source. In a group situation less individual energy is required. Teamwork is important. If a group functions well, the group members can assist one another when the demands become too much for any one person. Assistance comes in many forms. Sometimes it is a matter of helping one another with the work that needs to be done. At other times, it is subtler and involves helping others to regulate work or to recognize when breaks need to be taken.

What has been discussed to this point places responsibility for managing energy on the shoulders of workers. Another way to look at the situation is to consider the responsibility of employers for ensuring that workloads are reasonable. I have been involved with a colleague in evaluating an innovative workplace renewal project in Sweden. After a careful consideration of their situation (the needs of workers as well as finances), they reduced the workload by twenty-five percent for one year while keeping salaries intact. The requirement was that people take away twenty-five percent of their current workload and replace it with a project of their own choosing. This project could be personal such as getting into better physical shape or it might involve work on a research project that was of interest. The preliminary results were very promising. Sick days were dramatically reduced and members were enthusiastic about the impact on both their personal lives and work. In the second year of the project, some reductions were again possible but not at the same twenty-five percent level. It was interesting to note that the effects of the project were longer lasting than just the one year. Some behaviors in the workplace began to change even at the planning stage, as people began to think about their life and work situations. Also at the end of the year, changes in orientation seemed to be continuing. During my time with them, I observed staff doing aerobic exercises during the day as a continuation of their awareness of health in the workplace, stopping to share lunch together, and engaging in learning new skills with renewed energy.

125

Of course, not all workplaces are in a position to offer a twenty-five percent reduction in workload. But we are all in a position to evaluate lifestyle and workplace environments with a view to health and balance. In some situations it is helpful to offer more flexibility in working hours. Allowing people to work at home, where that is a possibility, can reduce stress in the workplace (and in the transportation corridors of our cities). Creating work environments that understand not only human potential but also human need and sometimes even frailty goes a long way to ensuring that the best job is done at the end of the day. The key variable is flexibility and personal choice. Workers with input into the structure of their working lives have less stress and are more productive with their time. Organizations also can help workers by developing work / life balance programs to help people cope with stress in their lives. Hobson, Delunas, and Kesic (2001) suggest that employees appreciate these organizational efforts; this appreciation further helps to promote motivation, productivity, commitment, and loyalty.

Efforts by employers to create a healthy work environment have tangible benefits. Kalbfleisch and Wosnick (1999, p. 17) point to the fact that workplace wellness "comes in the form of fewer insurance and workers' compensation claims, decreased absenteeism, lower turnover and higher productivity."

Energy Re-generation

While energy management is certainly a worthwhile goal, what happens in situations where the temperature drops to a level where it cannot be easily regenerated (burnout)? The reduction in temperature can become chronic. Certainly rest provides some relief, but eventually even rest is insufficient to rebuild our energy resources.

Regeneration of the energy source often requires a step backward before one is in a position to move forward. To understand this process of generating energy by moving backwards before moving forward, let us return to physics. Consider the movements of people as they try to generate energy in order to move an object forward. Think about the carpenter swinging the hammer back in order to hit a nail or the golfer's measured backswing before hitting the ball. In both of these instances, and in many more, power and energy come through the **backswing**, a measured activity where a goal is always in focus. For maximum success the backswing is followed by full contact with the object and a smooth follow through.

As people experience discouragement and frustration in their lives (moving towards burnout), they lose the will to press forward. In this frame of mind, there is little point in pushing ahead with decision making and action

127

planning. What is needed is a systematic review of past skills and accomplishments (the backswing) and the rebuilding of self esteem and confidence. The backswing provides momentum and with this regeneration of energy, there is the opportunity to move forward with hope and power.

Past Accomplishments

Psychologically, an important step in building the backswing is to return to past accomplishments. By assessing past events in a positive and constructive manner there is the possibility of seeing oneself in a new light. These remembrances are not simply a recounting of the past; they also include a careful analysis of the skills and personal qualities that are reflected in these events. Some questions that have been developed by Gray Poehnell and myself (Amundson & Poehnell, 1998) will help to guide this review. Start by identifying one specific accomplishment. Then ask yourself the following questions about the event:

Accomplishment:

1. What helped to make the event so successful?

2. Why did you do it? What was important to you?

3. What personal characteristics did you use?

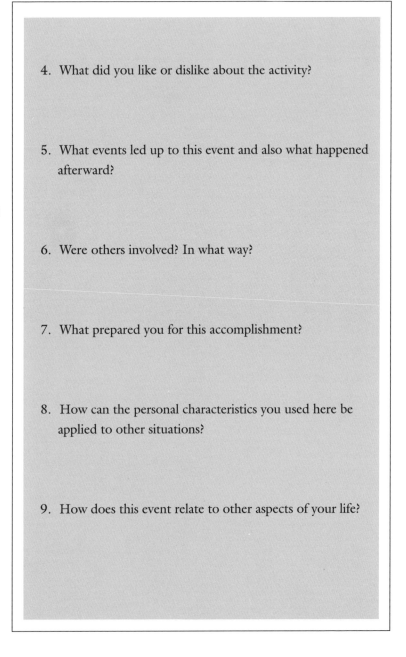

4. What did you like or dislike about the activity?

5. What events led up to this event and also what happened afterward?

130

6. Were others involved? In what way?

7. What prepared you for this accomplishment?

8. How can the personal characteristics you used here be applied to other situations?

9. How does this event relate to other aspects of your life?

By examining accomplishments in depth, you bring to mind many of the strengths that you possess. These strengths can act as heat sources that you may have forgotten you had, that may have been neglected in the busyness of your day, or that you may not have even realized you have. Sometimes it is useful to involve other people in this process of re-examination. Other people may see strengths that you have overlooked.

Hopefully this examination of accomplishments can give you some new ideas to reflect upon. Perhaps there is something here that also needs to be put into action. With the additional insights that you have developed, what needs to be done about it. If some concrete action is needed, take the time to write down your plan of action.

Action Plan

7

ELECTRICITY

*... a sense of life direction is as much about
what is outside oneself as it is about what is inside ...*

*... it is both the flow of energy and final destination
that provide a sense of life satisfaction ...*

*... one of the key tasks in getting energy flowing again is to
challenge some of our assumptions and perspectives ...*

134

Another form of energy transfer occurs when electrons actually leave the atoms to which they are connected and move to a new location. This movement is the result of magnetic attraction and is the foundation of electricity. The electrons, which have a negative energy field, move along magnetic lines toward the positive charge. This transfer of energy (electrons) from one object to the other occurs easily with some substances and not at all with others. Copper, for example, is a good conductor; wood, plastic, and glass are not. In general, the electrons in copper are not as tightly bound to the centre of the atoms and, therefore, move more freely. Consequently, we rely on certain metals like copper with high conductivity for the transfer of energy.

We have also learned to regulate the flow of energy so that energy moves along a specified pathway at a rate that does not overload the system. To control this flow, we use switches that determine when the energy flow will operate and when it will not (i.e., light switches serve this function). There also are fuses for protection that will shut down the flow of electricity when too much energy is passing through the system.

ELECTRICITY

As I have reflected on energy as electricity, I see that much of what has been discussed in the previous chapter on energy transfer can be applied here. There is, however, one important difference. Rather than random activity, the movement of electrons has a definite direction. It is this point that I would like to explore for parallels in the psychological domain.

There are many ways to think about having a sense of direction or focus. It can be as simple as having a preference for a certain type of ice cream or as complex as having a sense of life purpose or mission. In the light of the strength of magnetic pull and the clear sense of focused movement, I am inclined to consider direction using a deeper perspective, as with the discussion of the depth issues in Chapter Two.

Arriving at a sense of life purpose is not easy. A sense of direction is as much about what is outside oneself as it is about what is inside. Certainly we need to define our own particular electrical charge, but we also need to be searching for the complementary charge outside of ourselves. Gordon Smith (1999) defines the search for the external charge as a question, "what are the needs that we perceive in our world?" This is not just a question of needs. Rather it is needs, which are endless, in the light of who I am and where I am. It may be difficult to put into words what we personally see as the needs outside ourselves. To help us frame the question more clearly, Smith (1999), following the work of Kegan and Laslow (2001), suggests that it can be helpful to come at the issue from another perspective. Rather than thinking about the needs that you perceive, think about your complaints. (This is not about whining, the chronic complaining that we are all familiar with and probably guilty of at some point in our lives.) A healthy complaint not only identifies what is wrong but also indicates what we consider to be important. For example, if someone's complaint was about how people treated staff members who were lower in the organizational hierarchy, this may reflect a basic belief in the importance of justice and human dignity. It would follow then that as they looked at the needs of the world they might have a focus on issues of injustice.

To fully address an external need, we must match our personal abilities and interests with the resources that are available to us. Attaining this self-knowledge is an important component in developing a sense of life purpose. In earlier chapters, I have suggested ways to understand the patterns that help to define our lives. What hasn't been discussed as much is the integration of who we are with the needs that we perceive in the world.

There are many challenges associated with setting a life purpose. For some people, there is the tendency to focus too strongly on the self, while for others there is the over emphasis on the needs of the external world. People who only look inward run the risk of adopting a narrow and self-centered perspective, often described as neurosis or narcissism. The denial of self, on the other hand, can also lead to problems. People who only look outward lack the self-knowledge of how best to give themselves to the needs at hand. Their actions frequently turn out to be inappropriate to the need and unfulfilling for the individual.

The combination of self-understanding and external need brings together the fullest expression of energy flow. In this process, satisfaction is not solely defined by the end product. Joy is as much in the journey as in the end result. It is both the flow of energy and the final destination that provide a sense of life satisfaction.

For the most part, if we engage in activities that we consider meaningful, we are less inclined to feel overburdened and run the risk of burnout. This is not to say, however, that we can proceed with reckless abandon. As with the flow of electricity we need switches and fuses to help control the flow of energy. We need to take "mental health" breaks and to monitor our energy levels. Think about the situation you are in at the moment. Are you engaged in meaningful activities; and, if so, are you operating with the necessary checks and balances for your energy to flow smoothly? If not, what needs to happen to create meaning and balance in your life? We are back to the same issues that were first raised in Chapter Two.

Unblocking and Directing Energy Flow

In trying to achieve and maintain appropriate levels of energy flow, we may need to challenge some of our assumptions and perspectives. False self-messages, most often negative but periodically of a grandiose nature, may be blocking our pathway. Negative messages are particularly strong in situations where we have lost hope or self esteem. One of the key tasks in getting the energy flowing again is to challenge some these negative messages.

Challenging negative messages can proceed in a number of different ways. I have found it helpful to guide reflection and self-exploration with a set of questions. You may employ considerable flexibility in using these questions; the main point is that the various topics are covered. The questions that I have found helpful in challenging negative messages are as follows:

1. **Confirming Evidence:** What information supports the message? Rather than beginning with a challenge, I think it is important to allow for a full explanation of what supporting evidence there is for the message.

2. **Contrary Evidence:** What information runs counter to the message that is being examined? I have found that most negative messages can be exposed by ensuring that a full range of information is considered.

3. **Development over Time:** When and how did the message first begin to find a foothold? Using a timeline perspective, you can plot when the negative message first emerged and how it developed over time.

4. **Perception of Others:** How do others view the situation? Would others agree or disagree with the message? Negative messages find support and contradiction through interactions with other people. It can be helpful to explore these various interactions and perspectives.

5. **Impact:** How is this message affecting you? Once the exploration has been completed, the focus shifts to the overall psychological and physical impact of accepting a negative message.

6. **Desire for Change:** In light of your examination of this message, are you interested in making a change? If so, what? Ultimately the questions that have been asked

lead to a consideration of whether there is a desire to move in a more positive direction (i.e., to set aside the negative message and replace it with a more positive one). Of course, this then leads to a plan of action.

The activity that follows allows space for challenging a negative self-message. Hopefully, as you consider each of the following questions, you will arrive at a broader understanding how to move in a more positive direction. There may be more than one negative message that needs to be questioned. This process of challenging messages has the capacity to remove constrictions and generate positive energy.

140

Challenging Negative Messages

Identify a negative self-message that you tell yourself frequently. Examine this message by asking yourself the questions listed below:

Negative Self Message:

Questioning:

1. Confirming Evidence:

2. Contrary Evidence:

3. Development over Time:

4. Perception of Others:

5. Impact:

6. Desire for Change:

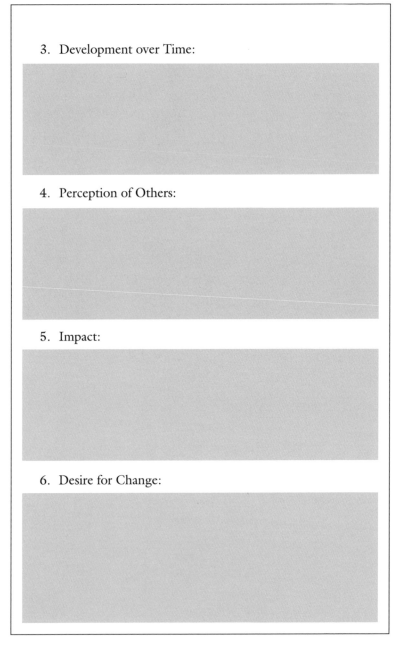

Another way to unblock and redirect energy flow is to change the metaphors we use to define ourselves. Metaphors are the word pictures we use to describe the ways in which we understand ourselves and the world in which we operate.

The questioning method described above can be applied to metaphors as well as to negative self messages. Suppose for example that you see your situation as hopeless and feel that you are "riding a roller coaster in the dark and the operator has fallen asleep." In reflecting on this image, you would start by listing the situations that have made you feel like this, and then describe those times when this wasn't the case. Following this lead, you might think about how long you have felt this way, when it started, and where you see it heading. Also, how do other people view your situation and what are your thoughts about their perspectives? Finally, what is the impact in your life of feeling this way, how satisfied are you with the situation, and how might you change the metaphor to make it more positive? Perhaps something needs to be done (by yourself or others) to wake up the operator or to turn on the lights. Also, are there any opportunities to get off the roller coaster and move to a new ride or even to pull the plug and stop the roller coaster altogether? As we dialogue with the image, we gain new understanding and renewed energy for action.

Questioning Metaphors

Take a moment to create a metaphor (a word picture or a drawing) for your life and then ask it the necessary questions.

Metaphor

Questioning:

1. Confirming Evidence:

2. Contrary Evidence:

3. Development over Time:

4. Perception of Others:

5. Impact:

6. Desire for Change:

At another level, we can completely change our metaphors to create new possibilities. Combs and Freedman (1990, p. 32) make a compelling case for moving in this direction. "Any single metaphor is a particular version of a particular part of the world. When people have only one metaphor for a situation, their creativity is limited. The more metaphors they have to choose from for a given situation the more choice and flexibility they have in how to handle it. Finding multiple metaphors expands the realm of creativity." I have found the work of Kerr Inkson particularly helpful in this regard (Inkson & Amundson, 2002). He has identified a series of what he calls "archetypal metaphors." These metaphors reflect different perspectives we can apply to any situation. Described below are some of archetypal metaphors that Inkson has identified.

1. **Journey:** viewing one's life as a pathway, an adventure, perhaps a pilgrimage.
2. **Inheritance:** looking at life as a gift, from the perspective of something given.
3. **Fit:** assessing the overlap between options and who you are as a person.
4. **Seasons:** using a predictable sequence of events (spring, summer, fall, winter) to describe change.

5. **Growth:** focusing on learning and developmental changes that occur over time.
6. **Works of Art:** viewing life tasks as projects requiring imagination and creativity.
7. **Resource Management:** seeing life as potential that can be organized and supported for maximum results.

Can you identify the metaphor you described earlier within this archetypal format? Also, how might your situation look if you change to other metaphors? Suppose for example that you are describing your situation as a journey down a turbulent river. How might the situation change if you considered it from the perspective of growth? Perhaps from this new viewpoint, the more difficult times can be understood as a necessary part of learning and life development. Using a resource management focus, the emphasis might shift to potential value or the need for greater control or direction (perhaps a motor for your boat) over life events. Whatever the outcome, the challenge here is to consider alternate metaphors so that your creativity and energy flow is enhanced.

Shifting Metaphors

In the space below, write the metaphor you identified earlier, identify some alternative metaphors, and then describe any new insights that emerge as you look at your life from the new perspective.

Metaphor:

Alternate Metaphoric Perspective:

New Insights:

As you come to the end of this chapter, can you see any action steps that can be taken to change or increase or possibly even regenerate your internal energy flow? Take a moment to identify the need and to develop the action steps that you will take.

Action Plan

8

H_2O:
HOPE, HEROES &
OPPORTUNITY

... with hope, no matter what problems we face today,
there are new possibilities for a better tomorrow ...

... we need to embrace the dream of the heroic
and use this momentum to push aside
the darkness of despair and cynicism ...

... the best opportunities come with the determination
to live a balanced life ...

The end of each chapter has had a focus on self-assessment and the opportunity to consider some type of action. If you are in a position to contemplate some type of life change, it is important that you go forward with attitudes that will complement the desire for something new. This chapter focuses on attitudes that will enhance and encourage change. For some the changes may be small; for others they will have much greater significance. The greater the depth of our personal investment, the more likely is the potential for lasting change.

I have identified three elements as a focus for attitudes that encourage and promote renewal and change. These elements are hope, heroes, and opportunity. As I looked more closely at these three concepts, I realized that I had the symbol for water, H_2O. Organically, water is the basic nutrient for life. It is essential. From an energy perspective, water can be a source of great power. Water also plays an important role in terms of movement and transportation. Symbolically water is used universally to speak of things that matter. Spiritually, water represents life and holiness, even in places where the water is no longer pure in and of itself. I think it is appropriate to incorporate the symbol of water into our ideas about change and the need for multi-dimensional action.

As you move toward action, you need to think about your physical needs for nourishment, power, and movement. Nourishment does not simply refer to the physical body; it also applies to our psychological and spiritual space or being. Are you taking the time to really nurture your self? Do you get the rest you need, stimulation from meaningful activities, and the support from other people? Is your spiritual space a well-tended garden, or is it like a desert or a place overrun with weeds and neglect? These are all important elements for growth and development. Power is the force that comes when you know your self and have a clear and positive plan of action in light of that self-knowing. Do you have the courage and the drive to take risks, meet challenges, and move forward in new directions? Are you actively directing your personal and career actions or just standing on the sidelines? As for movement, have you started the process of change; have you taken that important first step? If you have overcome inertia and are in motion, the next steps will come so much easier. Hopefully, your next steps will be enriched through consideration and application of some of the concepts associated with hope, heroes, and opportunity.

153

Hope

The renowned philosopher, author, and educatior, Henri Nouwen focuses many of his writings around the theme of hope. He uses the following quotation in describing some of the basic elements associated with hope: "Hope is an attitude. Daring to stay open to whatever today will offer, or tomorrow … that is hope. To go fearlessly into things without knowing how they will turn out, to keep going on even when something doesn't work the first time, to have trust in what you are doing" (in Durback, 1989, p. xvi).

First, there is openness, a willingness to consider a wide range of possibilities and opportunities. This openness is not a one-time event; it is something to be cradled through every stage of our life. Hope is willing to look beyond today and its events. It is a call to action, to go forward even in times when the outcome is not certain. Along the way, there will be failures and times when we "fall and skin our knees." With hope, we continue to press forward, trusting the path we follow and our ability to ultimately achieve success. Hope is full of courage, a word that will come up over and over again in this chapter. Here hope has the courage to walk through our fears. Hope is a life-breathing entity that can hold all of our positive action.

H$_2$0: HOPE, HEROES & OPPORTUNITY

People who maintain a high degree of hope are more likely
to be successful at many different levels, such as health,
general happiness, and achievement (Peterson, 2000).
Hope contains within it two sets of beliefs: first, the
assurance that there will be ways around whatever obstacle
or difficulty we encounter and, second, in a similar but
slightly different vein, the belief in one's own ability to
solve problems and achieve results (Snyder, 1994). The
first belief contains within it a sense that we operate in a
world where there is a force or forces bigger than ourselves.
While we may have different viewpoints about the exact
nature of this force, there is the belief that somehow things
will work themselves out for the good. The second belief
goes on to focus more specifically on our part in the
working out of this grand plan. Our effort matters and, if
we apply ourselves through hope-filled action, we will make
a difference. The combined strength of these two beliefs is
powerful.

155

As I have reflected on the concept of hope, I have tried
to identify some of the ways in which hope is built. At an
individual level, hope seems to be built when people ...

- are aware of and develop confidence in their own
  abilities and skills,
- have access to information that is helpful,
- see purpose and meaning in their efforts,

- believe that goodness exists as an ultimate reality,
- feel that they have responsibility for their own decision making,
- believe that they can make a difference, and
- are supported and encouraged in their efforts.

At a societal level, hope is built when people see ...

- leaders that care for the welfare of others,
- people making decisions who have the skills and attitudes to do a good job,
- follow through and consistency from leaders, promises made and kept, and
- leaders who have positive and possible visions for the future.

Cultivating a climate of hope is something that serves as a foundation for effective living (Jevne, 1991). Hopefulness seeks to flow through every aspect of our being. I have learned to listen for hope as I dialogue with people all over the world.

People with hope seem to be able to express thankfulness in the face of problems. Some of the "hopeful" statements I have heard from people who are unemployed are as follows: "Thankfully, I still have my health. I am sure that something will come along"; "We are going to be a bit short of cash for awhile but at least we

have each other"; or "It could have been worse, at least I
have some severance money to keep me going for awhile."
Being filled with hope does not mean that problems will
disappear. It means that we are prepared to live all of life,
the good times and the bad, on the other side of despair,
away from the cynicism that is its voice. We live with the
search for goodness, for wisdom, truth, and beauty,
knowing that with hope, no matter what problem we face
today, there are new possibilities for a better tomorrow.

157

Heroes

In the previous chapter, we spoke of metaphors and the
important role they play in shaping our lives. There is a
tendency to think of the heroic only as a metaphor for our
life rather than the real stuff of living, which it can be when
it is kept in touch with hope and opportunity. A closer look
at the heroic reveals that the characteristics usually
associated with heroism have much to do with the
spectacular and very little to do with true heroism. But, as
Michelle Tocher (1998) illustrates, there is another way to
look at this idea. Heroes most often start out as very
ordinary people. They don't necessarily have ambitions to
be or do something special. What sets heroes apart is that
they are hopeful and pay attention to their inner yearnings

for change and sometimes for adventure. They believe in something and are willing to move forward even though they can't always see what lies ahead. When obstacles occur, they try to find their way around the barrier, to keep going. At times, heroes run into trouble and need help from outside of themselves. They have doubts and feel like quitting; but they persevere, learning from their mistakes and applying their new insights. Courage is frequently a part of this perseverance. From this perspective, most of us can identify people who we might consider to be heroic. These people may be at various stages in their life; perhaps they are just beginning a new journey or perhaps they have had some tough times and are courageously trying to rebuild their lives. Some heroes are very young; others have a lifetime of happenings to look back on.

Another way to look at heroes is to consider the nature of the heroic journey, perhaps the most apt metaphor for this approach to life. Listed below are some defining characteristics:

- New possibilities emerge in challenging situations.
- There are difficult choices to be made.
- Commitment is part of maintaining a wholehearted focus.
- Synchronicity seems to be as important as planning.
- There are tests of readiness along the way.

H$_2$0: HOPE, HEROES & OPPORTUNITY

- People appear who help with the challenges of the journey.
- There are often "dragons" to defeat. Some are internal (fears, doubts); others are external (people, circumstances).
- At times, the "darkness" is real and threatens to be overwhelming.
- Reflection and personal development often occur during the journey.
- Some form of celebration marks the end of the journey.

Can you identify someone in your life who has lived heroically at various moments in time, people whose life or actions qualify them in some way as a "hero"? What would happen if you looked at yourself through the same lens? Can you find the "hero" that lies within you and affirm or re-affirm that capability? I think we need to embrace the dream of the heroic and use this energy to push aside the darkness of despair and cynicism. Being a hero is not something that is only reserved for special people. It is something that is available for everyone.

Heroes are not born overnight. Every heroic journey begins with a first step. There will be challenges along the way, but perhaps it is time to listen to the call to adventure. Consider the words of Henry David Thoreau and Mark Twain as inspiration in this regard:

"What lies before us
and what lies beyond us
is tiny compared to what lies within us."

- Henry David Thoreau

"Why not go out on a limb.
That's where all the fruit is."

- Mark Twain

Opportunity

The "call to adventure" and opportunity comes in many forms. The opening song of Bilbo Baggins from *Lord of the Rings* reflects some of the mystery and momentum of taking that first step.

The Road goes ever on and on
Down from the door where it began.
Now far ahead the Road has gone,
And I must follow, if I can,
Pursuing it with eager feet,
Until it joins some larger way
Where many paths and errands meet,
And whither then? I cannot say. (Tolkien, 1966, p. 48)

H₂O: HOPE, HEROES & OPPORTUNITY

As we walk (and run) along the pathways of life, we will face many challenging situations. These challenges present opportunities as well as barriers. Our willingness to take opportunities, that may present themselves as problems as much as they do as opportunities, will depend on how well we are connected to hope and the courage and humility of living heroically. Opportunity is a perspective growing out of our personal attitudes.

There is a tendency to see opportunity only in the light of chance events, "luck" as we have come to name this thing. Perhaps there is some truth here but it is important to also recognize a large element of personal investment. Mitchell, Levin, and Krumboltz (1999) indicate that learning to take advantage of opportunities depends on two principles: 1. willingness to explore new situations; and 2. the timely application of personal skills and qualities such as curiosity, persistence, flexibility, optimism, and risk-taking.

Many opportunities have as their starting point an engagement in some purposeful action. Take for example the person who decides to go back to school and acquire some new skills. This learning and accreditation help set the foundation for future work opportunities. Educational training does not guarantee a job at the end of the training period; it does put a person in a better position to take advantage of work opportunities. Of course, these opportunities do not always emerge at the end of the training program. Sometimes they come earlier and in other instances people have to follow other pathways or relocate before the journey can continue.

In my own life, I have seen many opportunities that appeared and disappeared as I let them fall through my fingers. Frequently they were simple doors to be opened or not in the course of a day. At times, this opportunity seemed to come with almost mystical power. Time for another story. I periodically buy lottery tickets to add to the birthday cards I give to my father. In one situation, I had a dream and, in that dream, saw the Lotto 649 balls falling down the chute. What stood out was that all six numbers were between 1 and 15. As I fell out of bed and scurried about the house getting my day organized, I set the idea of Lotto numbers aside, and asked my wife to buy the tickets when she would be out. On the drive to work, the dream continued to invade my thoughts and so I called home a little later. The tickets had already been bought, but my wife encouraged me to buy my own set of tickets and I had every intention of following through. And then came the busyness of work! At the end of the day, I realized that the time for buying tickets had passed. I put this out of my mind and carried on with my usual schedule.

H$_2$O: HOPE, HEROES & OPPORTUNITY

Later, while standing in a postal line, I glanced at the results from the previous week's Lotto. The results were exactly as I had foreseen! I have tried on other occasions to repeat the dream, obviously without success. Mystery, providence, an inner voice that doesn't take kindly to "busyness," is sometimes a part of what we simply define as opportunity.

It would be easy to dwell on the times that opportunities have not been acted upon. But there are also times when I did take full advantage of the opportunities that came my way. I have noticed that I am best able to create and respond to opportunities when I have balance in my life. Going back to the earlier dimensions of length, width, and depth, I find that maintaining balance in all three domains is of critical importance in developing and maintaining a flow of energy that is able to respond to opportunities that come my way.

To maximize the power, energy, and wholeness that belong to hope, heroes, and opportunity, you may need to examine your own life. Is it running at full capacity or as a single trickle? Is it in danger of going dry? Hope, heroes, and opportunity are attitudes to live with, to be nurtured in the stuff of everyday living. The following exercise will encourage the growth of these life-giving attitudes.

Hopes

What are your hopes? Start small with hopes for today. Make a list of as many things as you can realistically hope for today. If you lived where I do, you might hope for sunshine and find yourself, as I do, looking to the southwest for breaks in the cloud that bring a promise of sun. In chapter 2, there was a reflective exercise in which you could list at least 20 activities you enjoy; in a similar manner here, see if you can identify ten things that you hope for today.

Things You Hope for Today

1.

2.

3.

4.

5.

6.

7.

8.

As you consider the list you generated on the previous page, ask yourself the following questions.

1. How do the hopes you have just identified add balance to your life?

2. What are the hopes over which you have some control? Of those that are within your grasp, what actions can you take today to give substance to what you have hoped for?

3. What ones appear to be beyond your power to control (like the weather)? What desires or goals are behind the hopes that seem to be out of your control. For example, my desire for sunshine often reflects my desire to be outdoors, to go for a bike ride and get some exercise and fresh air. As you think about your underlying desires and goals, are there other ways to come to fulfill them?

H$_2$0: HOPE, HEROES & OPPORTUNITY

Beyond today, what are the hopes that you carry in your heart from day to day, that express the things you dream about or long for? These may be more distant in scope but nonetheless are real and a valuable part of your life? It takes courage to name these hopes and to give them a name and a place in our consciousness. List those hopes you consider to be the most significant for you.

My Most Significant Hopes

1.

2.

3.

Look at this shorter list of your most significant hopes that you have just identified. Are they your hopes, or are they someone else's hopes for you? Take time to consider their validity for your current life journey.

1. Do any of these hopes relate to the first list of hopes for your day? As you fulfill the daily hopes, how will they bring you closer to realizing these weightier hopes?

2. Are any of your hopes tied to the past? Do any need to be acknowledged and then released to make room for new hopes for a new time. There is a time that is right to grieve over lost hopes and dreams, to forgive those who may have robbed us of hopes that were ours. This is not an easy task; if you are in this place, you may want to seek out the support of a counsellor or someone you know you can trust to walk with you through this part of your journey.

A PARTING WORD

I t is always difficult to find the right words for this part of the journey. In many ways, I have come full circle. From the outset, a focus on three-dimensional living has drawn me towards a life that is fulfilled through a balance of length, width, and depth. This balance extended into the development of both an individual and collective identity. Exploring the full measure of who I am remains an ongoing life process. I am particularly intrigued by the nature of my collective self. In the light of all that I meet in my travels, I gain a greater awareness of the shape of my identity. And then there is the pathway that I follow; sometimes I move forward with great gusto, and at other times I am learning to seize the power and gift of the reflective moment. When I think of quantum thinking and the majesty of the unknown and the uncertain, I feel that I am moving closer to a deeper understanding of myself and my journey. But then I think of some of the little ways that I am utterly inflexible, playing the same music over and over, never tiring of the same food, the deep comfort of the familiar that wants to hold me in one place. Perhaps as Toffler (1970, 1980) said many years ago, we all need a little stability in our lives to help us cope with an uncertain

A PARTING WORD

world. As I go about my work, I find many of the messages contained in the chapters on energy transfer and electricity to be vital. It is so easy to get caught up in the "helping game" and set aside family and friends. There is so much to be accomplished but at the same time care is needed for the caregiver. I am hopeful that many of the people who are struggling with burnout will find some meaning in the words I have written.

The end approaches. I am increasingly aware that my sense of nourishment, power, and movement comes from attitudes of hopefulness, the heroic courage of others and myself, and a growing willingness to follow where opportunity leads, to listen closely to that small inner voice.

As I move forward, there undoubtedly will be some moments of frustration. I embrace the perspective of Zander and Zander (2000, p. 14) as I think about possible challenges. "The frames our minds create define—and confine—what we perceive to be possible. Every problem, every dilemma, every dead end we find ourselves facing in life, only appears unsolvable inside a particular frame or point of view. Enlarge the box, or create another frame around the data and problems vanish, while new opportunities emerge."

Thank you for sharing my journey. Hopefully you have found some words of wisdom and inspiration along the way. I have identified and presented to you a number of physical principles with parallels to the psychological world. There are undoubtedly more to be discovered and explored. Perhaps you will be the one to discover and pass them on. I would love to hear your wisdom and your stories. Hopefully there will be new opportunities to meet as our journeys carry on. We part with words for the road written by Tolkien (1966, p. 1066) for his friend, Frodo Baggins at the end of his adventure.

> Still round the corner there may wait
> A new road or a secret gate;
> And though I oft have passed them by,
> A day will come at last when I
> Shall take the hidden paths that run
> West of the Moon, East of the Sun.

REFERENCES

Ainsworth, M.D.S. (1989). Attachments beyond infancy. *American Psychologist, 44,* 709-716.

Amundson, N.E. (1998). *Active engagement: Enhancing the career counselling process.* Richmond, B.C.: Ergon Communications.

Amundson, N.E., Borgen, W.A., Ehrlebach, A., & Jordan, S. (in press). Survivors of downsizing: Helpful and hindering experiences. *The Cancer Development Quarterly.*

Amundson, N.E. & Poehnell, G. (1998). *Career Pathways: Quick trip.* Richmond, B.C.: Ergon Communications.

Arthur, M.B., Inkson, K., & Pringle, J.K. (1999). *The new careers: Individual action & economic change.* London: Sage Publications.

Bartholomew, K. & Thompson, J.M. (1995). The application of attachment theory to counseling psychology. *The Counseling Psychologist, 23,* 484-490.

Bodanis, D. (2000). *E=mc2.* London: Pan Books.

Borgen, W.A. & Amundson, N.E. (1996). *Starting points with youth.* Victoria, B.C.: MEOST.

Bowlby, J. (1969/1982). *Attachment and loss. Vol I: Attachment.* London: Tavistock.

Bowlby, J. (1973). *Attachment and loss. Vol II: Separation.* New York: Basic Books.

177

Bowlby, J. (1980). *Attachment and loss. Vol III: Loss.* New York: Basic Books.

Combs, G. & Freedman, J. (1990). *Symbol, story, & ceremony.* New York: Norton.

Csikszentmihalyi, M. (1990). *Flow: The psychology of optimal experience.* New York: Harper Perennial.

Durback, R. (1989). *Seeds of hope: A Henri Nouwen reader.* New York: Bantam Books.

Feller, R.W. (1995). Action planning for personal competitiveness in the "broken workplace." *Journal of Employment Counseling,* 32, 154 - 163.

Frost, P. & Robinson, S. (1999). The toxic handler: Organizational hero—and casualty. *Harvard Business Review,* July-August, 97-106.

Frankl, V. (1963). *Man's search for meaning: An introduction to logotherapy.* New York: Washington Square Press.

Gelatt, H.B. (1989). Positive uncertainty: A new decision-making framework for counseling. *Journal of Counseling Psychology,* 33, 252-256.

Goldberger, N., Tarule, J., Clinchy, B., & Belenky, M. (1996). *Knowledge, difference and power.* New York: Basic Books.

Guindon, M.H. & Hanna, F.J. (2002). Coincidence, happenstance, serendipity, fate or the hand of God: Case studies in synchronicity. *The Career Development Quarterly,* 50, 195-208.

Handy, C. (1994). *The age of paradox.* Boston: Harvard Business School Press.

Hawking, S. (1988). *A brief history of time.* New York: Bantam Books.

Herr, E.L. (1999). *Counseling in a dynamic society: Contexts and practices for the 21st century.* Alexandria, VA: American Counseling Association.

Hobson, C.J., Delunas, L., & Kesic, D. (2001). Compelling evidence of the need for corporate work-life balance initiatives: Results from a national survey of stressful life-events. *Journal of Employment Counseling,* 38, 38-45.

Inkson, K. & Amundson, N. (2002). Career metaphors and their application in theory and counselling practice. *Journal of Employment Counseling,* 39, 98-108.

Jevne, R.F. (1991). *It all begins with hope.* San Diego, CA: LuraMedia.

Kalbfleisch, R. & Wosnick, R. (1999). Beyond skin-deep: Long viewed as a superficial solution, a growing number of employers are now looking at wellness as a wise investment. *Canadian Healthcare Manager,* 6, 16-25.

Kegan, R. & Lahey, L.L. (2001). *How the way we talk can change the way we work: Seven languages for transformation.* San Francisco: Jossey-Bass.

Lewin, R. & Regine, B. (2000). *The soul at work.* New York: Simon and Schuster.

179

Lopez, F.G. (1995). Contemporary attachment theory: An introduction with implications for counseling psychology. *The Counseling Psychologist*, 23, 395-415.

Markus, H. & Nurius, P. (1986). Possible selves. *American Psychologist*, 41, 954-969.

Martz, E. (2001). Expressing counselor empathy through the use of possible selves. *Journal of Employment Counseling*, 38, 128-133.

McCormick, R., Amundson, A., & Poehnell, G. (2002). *Guiding Circles: An Aboriginal guide to finding career paths, Booklet 1: understanding yourself.* Saskatoon, SK: Aboriginal Resource Develpment Council of Canada.

Miller, A.F. & Mattson, R.T. (1989). *The truth about you.* Berkeley, CA: Ten Speed Press.

Mitchell, K.E., Levin, A.S., & Krumboltz, J.D. (1999). Planned happenstance: Constructing unexpected career opportunities. *Journal of Counseling and Development*, 77, 115-124.

Moses, B. (1997). *Career intelligence.* Toronto: Stoddart.

Moses, B. (1999). *The good news about careers: How you'll be working in the next decade.* Toronto: Stoddart.

Peterson, C. (2000). The future of optimism. *American Psychologist*, 55, 44-55.

Poehnell, G. & Amundson, N.E. (2001). *Career crossroads: A career positioning system.* Richmond, B.C.: Ergon Communications.

Poehnell, G. & Amundson, N.E. (2002). CareerCraft: Engaging with, energizing, and empowering career creativity. In M. Peiperl, M. Arthur, & N. Anand (Eds), *Career Creativity: Explorations in the remaking of work* (pp. 105-122). Oxford: Oxford University Press.

Prigogine, I. & Stengers, I. (1984). *Order out of chaos.* New York: Bantam Books.

Reid, A. (1996). *Shakedown.* Toronto: Doubleday.

Rule, W.R. (1983). Family therapy and the pie metaphor. *Journal of Marital and Family Therapy,* 9, 101-103.

Saltzman, A. (1991). *Downshifting: Reinventing success on a slower track.* New York: HarperCollins.

Schlossberg, N.K., Lynch, A.Q., & Chickering, A.W. (1989). *Improving higher education environments for adults.* San Francisco, CA: Jossey-Bass.

Smith, G.T. (1999). *Courage & calling: Embracing your God-given potential.* Downers Grove, Ill.: InterVarsity Press.

Snyder, C.R. (1994). *The psychology of hope: You can get there from here.* New York: Free Press.

Tipler, P.A. (1991). *Physics for scientists and engineers.* New York: Worth.

Tocher, M. (1998). *Brave work: A guide to the quest for meaning in work.* Ottawa: Canadian Career Development Foundation.

Toffler, A. (1970). *Future shock.* New York: Bantam Books.

Toffler, A. (1980). *The third wave.* New York: Bantam Books.

Tolkein, J.R.R. (1966). *The lord of the rings*. London: George Allen and Unwin.

Trompenaars, F. (1993). *Riding the waves of culture*. London: Nicholas Brealey.

Wujec, T. (1995). *Five star mind: Games and puzzles to stimulate your creativity and imagination*. Toronto: Doubleday Canada.

Zander, R.S. & Zander, B. (2000). *The art of possibility*. Boston: Harvard Business School.

182

About the Author

Norman Amundson, Ph.D. is a professor of counselling psychology in the Faculty of Education, University of British Columbia. He has over twenty five years of experience as a counsellor educator and is the current editor of the Journal of Employment Counseling.

His publications include over 60 journal articles and several books including Active Engagement (winner of the 2000 Canadian Counselling Association Best Book award), Career Pathways, and At the Controls: Charting Your Course Through Unemployment (over 1 million in print).

Dr. Amundson has been a workshop presenter and keynote speaker for many different associations and conferences. His work has a significant national and international flavour and includes presentations in Sweden, Denmark, Finland, Iceland, Hungary, France, London, New Zealand, Australia, Israel, Poland, the United States, and China.

The ideas for "The Physics of Living" began with a keynote presentation at the international Going for Gold Conference in Vancouver, British Columbia. The book itself was written when Dr. Amundson spent a sabbatical year "travelling the globe" and working and learning in many different cultural contexts.

To Contact the Author

To contact Dr. Amundson:

Dr. N. Amundson
Faculty of Education
University of British Columbia
Vancouver, B.C. V6T 1Z4 Canada
Tel: (604) 822-6757 Fax: (604) 822-2328
Email: amundson@interchange.ubc.ca

To order *Physics of Living, Active Engagement, Career Pathways, Career Pathways: Quick Trip, Career Crossroads, Employment Counselling Theory and Strategies, Guiding Circles*, or other publications of Ergon Communications, contact:

Ergon Communications
3260 Springford Ave.
Richmond, B.C. V7E 1T9 Canada
Fax: (604) 448-9025
Email: info@ergon-communications.com
Website: www.ergon-communications.com